Stress Is Optional! How to Kick the Habit

A Practical Guide to Living Free & Clear

Adam Timm

M tivational PRESS
LEADERS IN GLOBAL PUBLISHING

Published by Motivational Press, Inc.
7777 N Wickham Rd, # 12-247
Melbourne, FL 32940
www.MotivationalPress.com

Manufactured in the United States of America.

ISBN: 978-1-62865-153-9

Contents

To my family-

you gave me wings to fly

To my friends at Communications-

thank you for your patience and support

To the citizens of LA-

you taught me compassion

Acknowledgements

So many helped guide the journey that led here, to these pages. I must make boisterous mention of those key people without whom this dream would never have unfolded.

Julie Zipper, thank you for your wisdom, playfulness and passion, and the gift of meditation! Jessica Colp, thank you for shining your light and showing the pathway forward. Sara Armendariz, thank you for giving so generously and selflessly—you are a true bodhisattva. Kristen Moeller, thank you for showing me how to disrupt the ordinary and get out of the way; your guidance was everything. Venu Alagh, thank you for your keen eye. Rosemary Sneeringer, The Book Nurturer, thank you for your loving attention that helped make this second edition so much more. Dana Lin, your editing prowess is legendary and your guidance essential. It is an honor to walk beside you on this journey.

Mom, Dad, Jesse, Angelie, Ben and Joe—the stars. I love you.

Reggie Ray, your words and wisdom have shaped the course of everything since the path emerged. This truth is indestructible.

And a huge thank you to everyone who helped the first edition become a bestseller. The word is spreading—freedom is here.

Chapter One

"There is no stress in the world,
only people thinking stressful thoughts."
—Dr. Wayne Dyer

An Invitation

This is a message of Hope. Of opportunity.
Of a wonderful world that is waiting.

This is an exploration into a world
that may be a mystery to you.

A world of less stress.

A world where, instead of feeling shoved here and there by the
circumstances around us, you get to choose.

Choose FREEDOM.

And instead of being enshrouded in
confusion and struggle,
this pathway to freedom can unfold in a natural and easy way.

Welcome to your stressful life.

Who knew it would be like this?

It seems like everywhere we turn, there's another layer. There's stress waking up on time, stress on the morning commute, stress at work, stress at home, and if you've got the side-gig that so many of us do, there's stress there too.

It can start to seem like Life = Stress, right?

What if it could be different?

"Different? Like how?"

What if, instead of feeling tense and anxious at the very thought of everything you have to do today, you could look forward to it, without fear?

What if the stress you feel each day didn't dominate your every waking moment?

What if...

. . . your relationships were easier?

. . . you had the time to spend doing what you wanted?

. . . you had the energy to get out of the house when there was time?

. . . . And there WAS time?

What if you could realize this reality without quitting your current job, without getting divorced, and without putting your kids up for adoption?

I know what you're thinking.

"I've tried everything."

"I have kids, two jobs, there's no way."

"There's no time to do more."

"Hopefully next year I could do something like that... "

"Who will take care of my family?"

"On what planet?"

"Whatever, dude."

"Yeah, right."

No, I'm not from Mars. And yes, YOU can do this.

You can live a life with more happiness, more freedom, and less suffering.

"SWEET! Sign me up!"

Before you begin your journey, go here to meet Adam in person:
http://www.liveazenlife.com/meetAdam

What Is Stress?

The reality is that chronic stress is killing us. It's ruining our lives. We have this life to live, and we're running around like a chicken with its head cut off. Is this how it's supposed to be? Until retirement? Until we break down? In short, stress can be seen as the difference between how things actually are and how we would like them to be. The size of the space between the two determines how much stress we feel in any given situation.

Take traffic, for example. Why do we get so angry when we hit the road and have to slam on our brakes at the stop-and-go? There may be several surface-level reasons: We hate being late; we value our time, and traffic seems to waste so much of it; the people on the road are so rude; we just don't like driving; and so on. Beyond these surface-level reasons, what is really going on when we see those brake lights in front of us and we're stuck on he freeway that looks like a parking lot?

We wish it were different.

We wish we weren't running late. We wish we weren't stuck in traffic—again! We wish we had some control over this situation in which we feel powerless.

And, depending on how badly we wish it were different, we experience varying degrees of stress. This stress is felt in different ways.

There can be the constant stream of "Why me?" type of thoughts.

There can be the instant onslaught of a tension headache.

There can be the fiery rage that just waits for something to tip it off—the driver who cuts you off, the sudden stop of rubbernecking looky-loos, the hesitation of a driver who prevents you from making that left-turn light, which causes a full-on, finger-waving, horn-honking, yelling-out-the-window blowout.

What causes us to react in such a way? Is there satisfaction in it? Do we enjoy being angry to the point of having a screaming fit? Could we react differently (or not at all) if we wanted to?

Many of us don't even realize we're in the midst of such a reaction until it's too late. It's like a tidal wave that we didn't see coming. One minute we're humming along to a favorite tune, and the next—BAM! Stressed out. Day ruined.

But not all stress is necessarily bad. You've heard the saying, "Pressure is what makes championship teams," referring to the fact that when we are under a certain kind of stress, we can actually perform at a higher level than at other times. By identifying the kind of stress that's harmful, we can take appropriate action to prevent its effects.

Acute Stress vs. Chronic Stress

Psychologists identify two kinds of stress: acute and chronic. Acute stress is relatively short-lived. It's what you encounter when faced with a novel learning situation, and it is actually good for you in the sense that it allows you to remember the event, be it positive or negative. This is the type of stress you experience when you're challenged to be your best, whether as a child about to make your first solo musical performance or as an adult faced with a demanding intellectual situation or a physical challenge, such as winning a basketball championship.[1]

Chronic stress is long-lasting. *This* is the kind of stress that kills. It occurs when you worry all month about how you're going to pay your bills, or when you dread going to the same old job every day, , or when the stress at work spills into your home and continues unabated with no end in sight. Chronic stress, instead of priming us for the big game or enhancing our focus to learn an important skill, can start to make us feel claustrophobic: always tense, depressed, disconnected, or generally unhappy with our lives.

Our bodies are well equipped to handle short bursts of acute stress. You could even call this "good" stress. This is how we rise to our best in times of pressure, or get the heck out of a dangerous situation without having to think much about it. After this burst of adrenaline, our bodies return to normal, and life continues.

Chronic stress is a bit different. When we are constantly on high alert, the stress hormones adrenaline and cortisol course through our system day after day, and we begin to burn out.

Exhausted, we can become depressed and begin to lose focus on the joyful aspects of our lives.

Our bodies are like a car that needs regular tune-ups. If the car has been pushed to the brink with no maintenance and little care, it will eventually break down, overheat, or its engine will simply seize up. When we don't take care of ourselves, it can result in a sudden heart attack or general malaise as everything feels like another obligation —even things that are "supposed to be" fun.

The same thing happens to women who put themselves last and their children, spouses, and jobs first. They feel guilty if they make themselves a priority; yet if they constantly over-give without replenishment, they become resentful and exhausted. Ideally, we all want to give freely from our hearts when our own tank is full. Then, giving is easy and natural—and it feels good.

The bottom line? When we push and push, something has to give! And the wear and tear caused by chronic stress affects both mind and body in a cascading downward spiral. As the bodys tires, overwhelmed by anxiety and tension, our feelings of well-being dissolve. As we are less able to derive happiness from our daily lives, we look in the mirror and judge what we see. We see the world through a lens of fear and sadness.

The prison imposed by chronic stress is temporary. There is a way out, and you are holding the key to freedom. We've only allowed it to creep up on us because we didn't realize we had a choice. The exercises and practices in this book will give you the tools to make the damaging effects of chronic stress a thing of the past.

But first I'll tell you how I became such an expert on this topic—by meeting the struggle head-on myself!

▌ My Story

I know stress. The suffocating, stifling, "I don't want to wake up tomorrow" type of stress. We were reluctant frenemies for years — I answered 911 calls for a living. During my career as a 911 operator, I transformed from a person dominated by stress in all areas of my life to one who is content, peaceful, and pursuing the path of my dreams.

Back in 2010, my life was a prison. All around me I saw signs of my discontent manifesting outwardly. Even the circumstances I sought to save me from boredom and unhappiness -the new job, new girlfriend, new place to live, and new college degree no longer provided excitement or fulfillment.

I suffered through suffocating relationships (both professional and personal), disciplinary action at work, road rage, and the physical symptoms of stress (acid reflux, ulcers, tension headaches). Everywhere I turned, all I found was more stress. Leaving work felt good for about a minute, until I remembered the stressful situation I'd be walking into at home. This was my life.

I was that guy on the freeway, yelling out the window, honking, cursing the traffic jam before me.

I was the rude police operator you spoke to when you just wanted some relief from the loud party down the street.

I was that disgruntled employee who made it a point to show everyone how disgruntled I was.

Like Grumpy Bear who was all storm clouds, some regarded me as "Angry Adam."

I would see the doctor regularly for stomach pain, only to be told nothing was wrong with me. "Take this Zantac and come back if the symptoms persist," the doctor would say. My chiropractor tried for years, in vain, to cure the constant headaches—headaches caused by my stressful life. How could she cure my life?

Things with my girlfriend were particularly bad. In what became the final months of our relationship, we fought regularly about little things, mostly because we were no longer compatible. It was clear my relationship was long overdue for a breakup.

I can't say I was even aware of how bad things had gotten until I started to slow down a bit. Not until I committed to a practice of meditating—sitting and breathing for a few minutes each day—did I start to see the choices I made each day that kept me trapped.

It was at the urging of my dear friend Julie that I signed up for her meditation class, the last "40 Days of Meditation" class that she was to teach in LA before she moved to Texas. I had read a bit about meditation over the years, and several people had recommended that I try it, but I never did. Now it was time. I signed up. I didn't see it at the time, but my life was ripe for major change. Like a freight train blowing through town, changes were coming.

> The body offers subtle clues in the form of intuitive "gut feelings," or other physical reactions to our environment that can show us our next steps.

Meditation is about reconnecting the mind with the body. So often we rush around completely invested in our thoughts. Like floating heads, we are disconnected from what it actually feels like to live our lives. The body offers subtle clues in the form of intuitive "gut feelings," or other physical reactions to our environment that can show us our next steps. When we listen to the voice within, the voice of the body, we begin to see life more clearly. This voice becomes louder as we practice something I call "The Breath of Freedom." You'll learn more about this in a bit.

> Within just ten days of practicing the breath of freedom, my insight was growing stronger.

Within just ten days of practicing the Breath of Freedom, my insight was growing stronger. My body began offering strong clues that something must change or my sleepless nights would continue. After several days of waking up in the middle of the night and guzzling Pepto-Bismol to keep the indigestion at bay, it was quite clear that I could no longer sleep next to this beautiful woman next to me. It was time to break up with my live-in girlfriend. The dread!

I'd contemplated it before but I didn't know how to do it. Would she flip out? Would she key my car? Would she be okay? It was the apprehension of not knowing what would happen that kept me stuck. I had been waiting for a sign, and for nights on end I'd felt the painful signs of stress right in my gut: Do it now or continue to suffer, my inner voice was telling me.

When I broke the news to her, it was every bit as dreadful as I thought it might be. But she ended up being just fine, and within two weeks she was settling into her new place.

With peace restored to my home life, I began enjoying my personal time again. Working on music as a Dj and producer, meditating, watching movies, drinking tea on the front step—all these pleasant pastimes came back into the mix. How had I forgotten to do the things that I most enjoyed? I was returning to me, and peace was the result.

There was still something holding me in a state of stress and tension, however. For the three years leading up to this moment, in addition to holding onto a difficult personal relationship, I'd been working on a side business, a web TV start-up that had initially shown signs of great success. "This is the project that will finally allow me to quit my day job!" I remember thinking. "No more working for The Man! Woohoo!" But in reality, the side project was adding stress to my life more than it was lifting my spirits.

In fact, now that I was single again, I was enjoying my free time quite a bit. So much so that something became quite clear: I had willingly given most of my free time to my side business, especially in the last year, in order to avoid the harsh reality that my relationship at home was not working. I had missed the fact that my business relationship wasn't working either.

As the weeks went by, my sight grew clearer and clearer. With my high hopes, had I really overlooked the fact that this business was failing?

This dawning clarity was like being given x-ray goggles that allowed me to see exactly why I stuck around all these years: I was attached to the idea of being an executive at an exciting new company. I was attached to the idea that my business partner was a visionary CEO. I was attached to the thought that after three years of investing sweat equity in this company, success was just around the corner.

In truth, the role I'd fallen into was "Customer Service/Damage-Control guy." When my business partner missed appointments, I called the clients, apologized profusely, and rescheduled them. Stuck in the pattern of avoiding my home life, I had put up with this arrangement and overlooked its dysfunction.

I was a compassionate person, and he was working hard; he was doing the best he could, I reasoned. But really, why was I partnering with someone whose values didn't resonate with my own? Seeing the truth beneath my hope and expectation, I could no longer freely give my time to this failing endeavor. I left the project.

So in just three months of daily meditation practice, I had left my girlfriend of three years, my business partner of three years, restored order to my household, and officially regained control of my life. I suddenly had much more free time. Joy became a natural part of my days.

In just three months, order was restored to my household. I suddenly had much more free time. Joy became a natural part of my days.

I got along much better with my coworkers, my friends, family and even my fellow drivers on the road. And by continuing my meditation practice, a new path rose from the ashes of my former life. This path has led me to work that I am passionate about, a balanced life full of love, and so much more.

> **The funny thing is that it didn't require much effort. I didn't have to strive heroically for achievement. I didn't have to sacrifice my life and happiness to usher in this new way of being.**

The main thing it took was the courage to drop everything that I had been clinging to for so long. Leaving the old way behind created space for the new way to emerge.

When I look at my life today, I am filled with a deep sense of gratitude. I am part of a large and loving family, which is growing more with each niece added. The work I choose to do as a Freedom Coach—helping those trapped by chronic stress to realize freedom, fun, and fulfillment—is rewarding and exciting.

My home is a sanctuary, truly peaceful. The people with whom I surround myself are positive and uplifting, and the world that is reflected back to me by the results of my actions resembles something of which I can be proud. I am fit, I am healthy, and my life is well balanced. That is no small feat, as you have seen.

As a speaker and expert in the field of stress relief, I offer programs that allow people around the world to break free from the daily grind—proven, simple practices that make a huge difference, and I have shared them with you in this book.

Companies seek me out because they know that stress drags on productivity and equals unhappiness. Sixty percent of all doctors' visits are stress-related! But it's not only a matter of productivity. Those who suffer from daily chronic stress miss out on the ability and confidence to contribute their ideas and innovations.

Stress limits them to a life of being in "coping mode," where enthusiastic engagement and creativity is impossible.

HERE'S WHAT I'M SAYING

–You don't have to go live on a mountaintop to get away from stress.

–You don't have to suffer from insomnia or wake up in the middle of the night with panic attacks.

–You don't have to stay numbed out, feeling like a zombie going through the motions day in and day out.

–You don't have to quit your corporate job to feel excitement and purpose again.

–Freedom is your birthright, and you can claim that freedom today!

–Right now, even though you may feel far away from your dreams, you can recover that peaceful sense of well-being, the delight and pleasure in simple tasks, the excitement of new experiences, and a dawning sense of purpose, if you can only commit to a few simple practices.

Your Journey Begins

All it takes to begin your own journey is an awareness of where you are now and the tools to get where you want to be. This book will help you find both.

It begins with some information that you may or may not know about:

– What stress is at the biological level

– What actually happens to our brains and bodies when we encounter a stressful event

– The effects of one day of stress vs. several years of stress

Some interesting things happen when we suffer from chronic stress. Did you know that stress is an underlying factor of six of the leading causes of death? Sounds like something needs to be done about this!

Here's the good news: Something can be done about this. Each chapter ends in a "See Through Your Stress" activity designed to increase your awareness of how stress is affecting you.

The final section of this book is a practice guide full of tips, tools, and techniques that you can start using today to feel relief from

> Did you know that stress is an underlying factor of six of the leading causes of death?

your daily stressors. When practiced on an ongoing basis, these techniques will change the way your brain and body act when stressed.

Things that once stressed you out won't anymore. Daily feelings of tension and anxiety will decrease or end altogether. You will reclaim your life and breathe easy again!

Sound good? Let's get to it!

Activity—See Through Your Stress

A Word About Journaling

This book is arranged as an exploration into the ways you relate to the stressful aspects of your life. As your exploration unfolds, it is helpful to have a journal or notebook handy to write down the discoveries as they come.

A journal will also give you a great place to write down your answers to questions posed in these "See Through Your Stress" activities throughout the book. Self-reflection is a powerful way to understand the inner workings of your mind and shed some light on why you respond to stress the way you do. Your journal is a mirror for this reflection.

Find a notebook that speaks to you. You will be looking at this book every day until it's full, so choose something that you like. I am partial to the Moleskine line of bound notebooks. They are sleek, well constructed with heavy paper and quality covers, and have an elastic band to keep them shut when not in use.

Once you find something that suits you, open to the first page and write a few words of intention, something to get the ball rolling. With each new volume, I like to start off with words about what's going on in my life, along with well wishes for what's to come   .

Adam Timm

Chapter Two

"The greatest weapon against stress is our ability to choose one thought over another."
—William James

What Causes Stress?

Several factors leave us particularly inclined to living a high-stress life in our fast-paced world. We are predisposed to a habit of stress-ful living because our species has evolved with one purpose in mind: survival. But what happens when our survival is not at stake? We can still be burdened by these survival mechanisms. They shape our worldview,and this worldview is not always beneficial.

When we understand how our brain responds to stress, along with the subtle states of mind that cause us stress, we can surf the wave of life instead of being tossed about like a ship on stormy seas. We can be in control of our lives, instead of being controlled by stressful events.

Five primary factors lay the groundwork for our habit of chronic stress:

1. The body's natural response system
2. Identification with Self vs. "Other"
3. Resistance to change
4. Pursuit of pleasure, avoidance of pain
5. Our own past conditioning

The following is a brief summary of each factor. We will get into this more deeply in the next chapter.

The Body's Natural Response

We are all too familiar with what it feels like to be stressed-out, but what makes us so susceptible to the stranglehold that stress has our lives? One reason why we have a propensity for stressing out lies in the physical makeup of our brains and the machinery behind what happens each time we perceive a threat.

Both the equipment used (the areas of the brain) and the stress response itself have evolved over the course of millennia. They have ensured the survival of our species. We have been prey to creatures higher up on the food chain for much longer than we've been sitting at the top as we are now.

Yet here we are, relaxing in our rather cushy modern lives, still responding to every stressor as if it were a life and death situation.

> To our brains, that traffic jam may be life and death. But we know better. And we can use our minds to change the way our brains respond to everyday stressors, employing specific practices to live with more peace, calm, and joy.

Identification with Self vs. "Other"

In addition to the fact that we are well equipped and quite conditioned over millions of years to respond to threats in a certain way, we hold viewpoints about reality that tilt us in the direction of a stressful existence. The first is our identification with self versus other. This viewpoint arose because it was necessary for the brain to determine the boundaries of its body in order to ensure the survival of the organism. In the field of immunology, this process is described as the cells determining "self" and "non-self" so that the body can fend off infection.

As we grow from just a few cells at conception to many millions more, this predisposition remains. We hold an inherent fear of others based on the need for survival, and on top of that we are taught to fear strangers as children. The more strongly we identify with self-preservation and the less we identify with other, the more we are ruled by fear. But we can change this viewpoint as we relax into seeing the deeper truth of reality. More on this later.

Resistance to Change

Another fact of reality that causes us anxiety is the presence of perpetual change. We spend our entire lives attempting to live comfortably—trying to get that stable job, putting money away for retirement, not taking too many risks. We hope for easy and secure circumstances that we can count on. We arrange our days according to the path of least resistance.

But these desires for security mask a deep fear of the unknown. As the old saying goes, "The only thing constant in life is change." This uncertainty can be unnerving. With practice, however, we can breathe confidence into this fear of change, find within ourselves the resources to overcome adversity, and boldly meet any unexpected moment of our lives.

> We spend our entire lives attempting to live comfortably.

Pursuit of Pleasure, Avoidance of Pain

Going along with this disdain for change and our attempts to shore up the uncertain avenues of our existence is our default setting of wanting to pursue pleasure and avoid pain. At work, we can see this in the way that everyone is so focused on the next day off, the next vacation. At home, we see this in the way we procrastinate and skirt household chores. We can even see it in the example of the traffic jam. We'd love to avoid the pain of being late and wasting time, and wish for the pleasure of a freely flowing freeway. This causes resistance – stress!

As we engage in what's become a lifelong pursuit of pleasure over pain, we experience stress when we are invariably met with pain.

> At work, we can see this in the way that everyone is so focused on the next day off, the next vacation.

We really can't avoid some aspects of pain in our lives, and the tricky thing is that pain is completely subjective. What you define as painful might not even register as pain for me, and vice versa. But again, with practice, we can accept all of life's ups and downs, deriving strength and confidence from that which does not kill us, while discovering that pain doesn't necessarily mean it's the end of the world.

Past Conditioning

We've mentioned evolutionary conditioning as a cause of stress sensitivity, but what about certain life experiences that have left us scarred? Traumatic events in early childhood can be particularly powerful in shaping the way our bodies respond to stress, as can extreme events later in life. Current research shows that even ongoing low-level chronic stress can leave us more vulnerable to future overwhelm at the hands of a stressful event. Though we've lived a certain way, responding poorly to stress possibly all our lives, it doesn't always have to be this way. We can deprogram these worn pathways of being and usher in an easier way. Within us is the power to turn things around, but we have to take the first step.

> Current research shows that even ongoing low-level chronic stress can leave us more vulnerable to future overwhelm at the hands of a stressful event.

▌Activity—See Through Your Stress

We often arrive at our state of being chronically stressedwithout even knowing it. It is all we have known up until now, and we can't solve a problem using the same mindset that created it. It's time to open up our thinking to see our patterns of behavior and thought that keep us tied down.

To begin to make room for a less stressed way of being, I am going to invite you to slow down a bit. Create some space in your life by doing one or more of the following:

- Leave earlier for work so you can take the long way.

- Take a brief (5-10 min) walk in the middle of your day.

- Look around you. See the trees blowing in the wind, the brilliant blue sky, the green blades of grass. Really take it all in.

- Smile more, for no reason (don't worry, no one will see—and if they do, you've just spread some joy!).

- Dance around your house.

- Disconnect from technology. How long can you go without looking at your phone?

The more often we take opportunities to approach life a little less rushed, to bring about feelings of happiness, the more we unplug from the reflex of chronic stress.

Begin using these suggestions today to pull the plug on the habit of stressful thinking. Track how often you use them, and jot down how you feel afterwards. Lighter already!

Chapter Three

"Slow down and everything you are chasing
will come around and catch you.
—John De Paola

▍ The Biology of the Body's Stress Response

When we understand how we behave when we're confronted with the stressful aspects of our lives, we're better able to change those reflexive reactions that lead us to experience detrimental and long-term chronic stress. One of the reasons we allow chronic stress to be such a dominating force in our lives is that it has become a way of life, and there doesn't seem to be a way out. We might not even be aware that our reaction to the day's stressors is unhealthy.

As this way of life has developed—our everyday response to stress—our brains have physically created neural pathways to process the stressful experiences.

> Much as in the case of addiction, these worn neural pathways cause us to quickly and easily respond in the same way each time a stressful event occurs. It's automatic—our response to stress has become a reflex.

In other words, we've become trapped—imprisoned—all by our own doing.

Even if that response is unhealthy, like when we yell or throw something out the window when someone cuts us off in traffic, we'll return to it again and again, unable to imagine behaving another way, even justifying such outlandish actions, "It's all their fault!"

The great news is that these neural pathways are not set in stone and can be changed. With awareness, we become creators of every moment instead of being swept away in a rush of angry emotions. We can change our relationship to the stress and tension that we have gotten used to. We can dream of a different way of being and make it a reality.

Stress, Evolved

Why has it proven so easy to fall into this pattern of behavior? Why is it so hard to see how our stress is dominating our lives? And once we see how stressed-out we are, why is it so hard to change our behavior? (Isn't it telling that some people need to suffer a heart attack before contemplating a life of less stress?)

The answers to these questions begin to unfold quite naturally when we look at the place where each and every one of our life experiences begins and ends: the brain. The brain, geared for survival, has evolved to protect us. Our default response, whether it's a thought or a reaction, has been conditioned by this physical evolution.

In the mid-1950s, Paul D. MacLean, an American neuroscientist, proposed a model to help explain the evolution of the human brain. MacLean's model became known as the triune brain, and it describes three evolutionarily distinct neuro-computers, each with its own intelligence, subjective feel of the world, and sense of time and space. The three brains work in a sort of daisy chain, each governing a certain aspect of our experiential reality, and as we will see, when one of the three brains is dominant in an individual at the expense of the others, it can be difficult to see beyond the constricted view offered by this dominant area.

According to MacLean's model, the first area of the brain to evolve was the R-brain, or the reptilian brain, which is primarily concerned with regulating the automatic functions of the body. Breathing, body temperature, heart rate, digestion—all the stuff that we never need to think about. The R-brain is also involved with the very beginnings of the stress response. If you've ever swum underwater for a bit too long and experienced panic over the possibility of running out of air, you're familiar with how the R-brain will react when the body's vital functions are threatened.

The next area of the brain to evolve was the limbic system, also known as the mammalian brain, or M-brain. The limbic system is the seat of our emotional and instinctual ways of reacting to our world—the home base of our "fight or flight" trigger. In the limbic system, signals to the brain are decoded according to four fundamental programs, known as the Four F's: fear, feeding, fighting, and fornicating.[2]

It is this area of the brain that is activated when we walk into a new room feeling a bit on-guard, assessing things before finally allowing ourselves to relax. This level of conditioned defensiveness will determine the severity of the stress we feel in a new situation. As we will see, if our typical reaction to life is to be on alert, over time we become less able to turn down this stress response, and we become more and more stressed as a result.

The most recent area of the brain to evolve, the area concerned with the higher brain functions, is the neocortex. It is involved with sensory perceptions, generation of motor commands (walking, waving "hello," skipping for no reason), spatial reasoning, conscious thought, and language. If we do not need to fear, fight, seduce, or dine with a person we encounter in any particular situation, the thalamus relays the sensory information, colored by the joys, excitements, worries, or concerns of the limbic brain, to the neocortex for reflection and appropriate behavior.[3]

The three brains are in constant communication with each other. The R-brain itakes care of the involuntary functions of the body, the limbic system regulatesour emotional situation, the neocortex allows us to move about the activities of our day.

Under normal circumstances, messages and impulses flow freely between all areas of the brain, and our day goes smoothly. As we walk down the street, relaxed, we breathe easily, noticing the beauty of the brilliantly shining sun.. We feel content, joyful. Our mind is clear.

When a stressful event occurs, however, something else happens. Communication between the three brains does not flow freely. Our bodies go into survival mode. Say you're walking down a dark street one night, enjoying the evening breeze, when you become aware of someone possibly following you. Your heart rate increases as cortisol and adrenaline are released into the blood stream.

These steroids, secreted by the pituitary and adrenal glands, give us quick energy, direct blood away from digestion and other non-emergency body functions, and reroute blood to our extremities and muscles so we can fight or flee. When this happens, our rational mind is largely bypassed as the older brains, the R-brain and the limbic system, take over.

This reaction to danger is ancient. You can see it in your neighborhood squirrel that is always on the run, foraging for food and then fleeing at the slightest movement. The fight-or-flight mechanism has kept our species and others alive over millions of years.

Our bodies evolved to handle short bursts of acute stress, like running from a saber-toothed tiger, and then relaxing in the comfort and safety of the cave. We're not meant to handle continuous bouts with chronic stress over money, work, family, bills, and on and on.

There is no doubt that in times of danger, this chemical influx is necessary to help us fight or flee, but we can get locked into a state

> Unlike acute stress, which serves a positive purpose, chronic stress is very destructive.

of chronic stress when the adrenal glands don't receive a signal to stop producing these hormones. Unlike acute stress, which serves a positive purpose, chronic stress is very destructive.[4]

In the last 15,000 years, our species has changed from tribes of hunter-gatherers who roamed the land in fear of predators, to large-ly sedentary populations living in cities. Our conditioned response to perceived dangers in today's world has the ability to create more harm than good.

The Three Bases of Stressful Thinking

Along with the biological machinery of the brain, we evolved three worldviews that create daily friction. Each one arose from the body's need for protection. Without these worldviews deeply ingrained in our very being, we might not be here today.

Becoming aware of how these ways of thinking affect our levels of daily stress, offers the opportunity to choose a different way of relat-ing to our environment, instead of the reflexive, fear-based wayswith which we were born.

These worldviews, in no particular order, are:

- Identification with Self vs. "Other"

- Resistance to change

- Pursuit of pleasure, avoidance of pain

Identification with Self vs. "Other"

In order to provide solid footing for understanding the world as we grew up, we learned to establish boundaries between inside and outside—the inside world, "me," and the outside world, "them," or "Other." This dualistic thinking is applied to everything we see, but is actually not real. The truth is that our brain has created this duality as a useful fiction, a survival advantage in times of split-second deci-sions. As a result of this dualistic thinking, we are taught to fear the "other," whatever that other thing might be.

Think of all the suffering that arises out of this fear: Prejudice and aggression of so many kinds, predicated on the idea that "I" am somehow more justified than "you." Buddhist tradition speaks of the origin of suffering as our continual struggle to try to preserve this idea of a definitive "self" at all costs. Based on our belief in a "self," if someone appears to ignore us or insult us, we will consider that person an enemyand will mobilize all the feelings, attitudes, and actions that we consider appropriate to someone who is against us.[5]

Our society is steeped deeply in this idea of individuality. We need the latest fashions to set ourselves off from the rest of the crowd. We strive and make heroic efforts to be better than the next guy. We are in constant competition with our fellow humans, seemingly competing for scant resources in an unjust world.

But are we really alone against the world? Have you ever examined how connected you are to your fellow humans? Just take a look around you. The clothes you wear, the food you eat, your work, your transportation—in every aspect of your life you can see the involvement of quite literally thousands of people spanning this and each generation that came before. There is no separation between us. We are all connected.

And the deeper truth speaks to this. We believe in a static and unchanging self,but the person we see in the mirror actually changes minute by minute. For example, 98% of all of the atoms that make up your body right this minute will be different in one year.

We think the brain is the only part of our body that holds conscious awareness, but really, every cell in our body is sentient and exists as a fractal of the larger whole. Each cell in our body has the ability to express the function of any other part of the body.

A brain cell simply has its "brain cell" attributes turned on. It could just as easily have been a bone cell. When looking at brain images of people who were asked to think of themselves by name, or some attribute that they feel defines them, several areas of the brain light up! So then, the self is just an idea, perpetuated by our need to hold onto something unchanging, something substantial, something "real." But what I call "Adam" is really just a collection of memories from the past, truly just a figment of my imagination.

As we grow into this identification with Self over "other," we become entrenched in defending this fiction. We feel the need to protect ourselves at any cost, especially when it comes to our ideas. This is another adaptation brought about by the organism's need to survive, but an over-identification with "Me" and "My view" creates stress and tension when we're deeply invested in our personal standpoint, taking personally things that aren't actually personal.

How many times have you taken issue with something that a friend is going through, getting all worked up over the injustice of the situation, even though the situation doesn't really even involve you? Really, how often can we be justified in taking situations personally? Even when something is meant to be a personal slight, we can choose to just let it go. If you were free from this "Me" versus "The World" mentality, how much in your relationships would change for the better?

Resistance to Change

Just as when we look in the mirror and see the ever-changing organism that is our body (yet we think we seesomething that is static and unchanging), we are wrapped up in a quest to find something solid and unchanging. We fear uncertainty—the mystery of the unknown can be unnerving. We like the comfort of a familiar blanket.

We know its smell, its feel; we've been there before, and we can count on it.

As the world around us spins at 1,040 miles per hour, we cling to the past in an attempt to bring some of its familiarity along with us. And like a relationship that's long overdue for breakup, we find that ideas from the past, while once providing a familiar blanket of feel-good protection, now constrict our ability to live the life we were meant to live.

We cannot avoid change, and this is scary. It produces anxiety and rampant thinking: "What if I fail?" "What's going to happen now?" "Why'd you do this to me?!" This fear leads us to surround ourselves with all sorts of distractions: TV, smartphone, iPad, relationship, hobby to keep the anxiety dialed down. How dialed down is it, though? Our baseline of "I can't sit still" is almost always with us. Can you feel that slight uneasiness in the background even now, as you read this sentence?

This fear of change arose from simple beginnings. Change, at times in our history, has meant great hardship. Think of how our early ancestors might have responded to the coming winters. If the changing of the seasons wasn't taken seriously, it could easily spell death for the entire tribe. Against the backdrop of this severity, these ancient indigenous peoples were required to plan far ahead. In fact, this is all the hunter-gatherer tribes did for thousands of years: they roamed the Earth in search of food and shelter in order to survive the next season and the next. If they didn't fear what was possibly to come—death—we might not be here today. This fear is written into our DNA.

Fast forward to modern times. We aren't in danger of the changing seasons or food shortages, but the ingrained fear of change still exists. Some of us even spend thousands of dollars on attempts to keep from changing and aging, i.e. plastic surgery. Fear of aging is a fear of change. Fear of aging is still that old-age fear of death, which is the ultimate change.

Change is here to stay. We are changing, the world is changing; we might as well go along for the ride. Resistance is futile; it causes stress. When we embrace change, or at least accept it, we can seriously dial down the amount of stress that is caused by change. How? It's easier than you think.

Change is here. We are changing, the world is changing; we might as well go along for the ride.

Pursuit of Pleasure, Avoidance of Pain

Just as we have a natural tendency to get stressed at the first sign of change, we are naturally inclined to pursue pleasure and avoid pain. This is another evolutionary holdover that has aided in the survival of our species. This tendency is the basis of the deep machinery of likes and dislikes. While it is only natural to form likes and dislikes as we progress on our journey through life, we encounter difficulties when we neurotically pursue of pleasure above all things, shunning everything that doesn't enhance our pleasurable enjoyment of the world. In this mindset, we begin to grasp at things we deem pleasurable and push away everything else.

This tendency is a slippery slope. How often do our likes and dislikes change? Clearly we don't find pleasure in the same things we did when we were in grade school or even high school, for that matter. Later in life we probably won't like certain things that bring us pleasure now.

> How reliable, then, is our determination that this thing
> that brings us pleasure today is "good" and should
> be pursued at the expense of something that we may
> judge as less pleasurable, which we deem "bad?" Not
> very reliable at all.

A Zen parable tells the story of an old farmer who had worked his crops for many years. One day his horse ran away. Upon hearing the news, his neighbors came to visit. "Such bad luck," they said sympathetically. "Maybe," the farmer replied. The next morning the horse returned, bringing with it three other wild horses. "How wonderful," the neighbors exclaimed. "Maybe," replied the old man. The following day, his son tried to ride one of the untamed horses, was thrown, and broke his leg. The neighbors again came to offer their sympathy for his misfortune. "Maybe," answered the farmer. The day after, military officials came to the village to draft young men into the army. Seeing that the son's leg was broken, they passed him by. The neighbors congratulated the farmer on how well things had turned out. "Maybe," said the farmer.

As the story illustrates, we can't actually know whether something is good or bad. If we cling to something we label "pleasure," and instead it brings pain, we've just set ourselves up for disappointment, suffering, stress.

When we derive a sense of self-worth from our ability to attract that which brings us pleasure—only to find that it no longer pleases us—who are we then?

The problem isn't that we have likes and dislikes, it's that we define ourselves through them. We make decisions based on limited information and changing tastes. We're passionate about certain things and cold towards other things. Sometimes we don't even know why, yet we chart a course in the direction of these passions—destination pleasure!—only to find out weeks, months, or years later that the oasis we sought was just a mirage. And when we derive a sense of self-worth from our ability to attract that which brings us pleasure—only to find that thing no longer pleases us—who are we then?

So much life is spent in pursuit of our personal idea of what pleasure is that we miss the journey. We hustle past all of the annoyances we meet along the way on our quest for the thing that will truly, once and for all, bring us the pleasure we seek. Even this can be stressful: the constant waiting, evaluating, and pushing away the things that don't live up to our ideal of comfort.

But we can expand our definitions of pleasure and pain, take a step back, and see a bigger picture. The bigger picture is less one of polar dualities—good/bad; pleasure/pain—and more of a constant ebb and flow. Some things bring pleasure, some things bring pain, and it's all good—if we can allow for it.

Sometimes pain spurs greater intention and fire. If you think you're going to get laid off, maybe you'll start looking for a better job. In this case, pain leads to "better." When couples are having issues, it's painful and hurtful, but if they can talk through the issues, they gain deeper intimacy and trust. This perceived pain leads to something good: greater bonding. Pain isn't always bad; it's a sign that something needs attention.

The final piece to understanding how we create and endure unneeded stress and tension has to do with our own conditioning since birth.

Our Own Past Conditioning

As we've grown, we've picked up many habits along our journey. Many are good things, and some are things that we'll spend our whole lives deprogramming. The beautiful thing is that every one of our reflexive responses have come about and remained a part of our life's toolkit because they served us in some way. Yet if we can recognize that some old habitsare now causing us more harm than good, then it's time to sever the ties with these worn-out ways of being. Some of our ways of responding to stress were wired into our brains at a very young age—even before we were born in some cases! Other ways have emerged through our gradual indoctrination into the culture we live in.

For the sake of survival, a child needs to develop an instinctive sense of potentially threatening situations. This is why, early in life, we develop aversions and fears in association with experiences that we perceive as dangerous. When a child under the age of seven experiences trauma, these traumatic events can be particularly powerful in shaping future perceptions of danger. During early years of life, the child's brain is like a digital recorder set on constant record. The brainwave frequency for a child from birth to age two is in the delta range, which is also the frequency of the brainwaves of a sleeping adult. The brainwave frequency for a child from two to six is in the theta range, which is what an adult experiences in a state of imagination or reverie or while dreaming.

Only around young adulthood does a child's brain become fully adult-functional, operating in the higher frequencies of the alpha and beta wave ranges. In other words, a child under seven years of age basically functions in a hypnotic trance or dream state, which allows that digital recorder in the brain to gather information—and form neural pathways —appropriate for the youngster's environment without the filtering and interference of logic and reasoning from the neocortex.[6]

When these early neural pathways are formed duringtraumatic experiences, these experiences create the basis for a predisposition to feelings of anxiety—in effect setting the stress response system at a level of hypersensitivity.

In my own childhood, there was a particular experience that shaped my approach to the world.

When I was growing up, my father's discipline was fierce at times. Between the ages of five and seven, my younger brother and I shared a huge bedroom that took up the entire attic level of ourhouse. Occasionally, on evenings when we were sent to bed and weren't tired, our large collection of stuffed animals became projectiles as we engaged in legendary animal fights, chucking our stuffed friends at each other from across the room. What fun! Until we heard the door to our bedroom open. Then the footsteps up the stairs. When did those footsteps begin to register as terror?

In the few moments that it took my father to come up the stairs, round the wooden banister, and reach our beds, we attempted to jump under the covers and pretend to be asleep, only to have the covers flung off, arms jerked, and spanking issued in an instant. The message: "It's time for bed!" I'm not certain how many times my brother and I were dealt with in this manner, but it was enough times to know that if we were caught horsing aroundafter bedtime, there would be a price to pay.

These events left an indelible mark on my developing brain. I fearfully interacted with the world as a young boy, with a timidity that I didn't outgrow until high school. I always had trouble falling asleep, most nights just lying in bed with my eyes open until I dozed off. I was always somewhat wary of my father for the way he ruled with fear, and I remained distrustful of people in general. I was fearful, anxious, always on alert: the signs of a hyper-vigilant stress response.

Values

What we value also has an impact on the amount of stress we experience. These values can come from our families, our friends, the organizations we grow up with, the cities where we live, and the society at large.

A great example is the way we value time. There's no question that the clock dominates our society. We are always checking it, waiting, feeling good about running on time, feeling rushed about running behind, always comparing how we feel against whether we're running on time..

But it doesn't end with the timing of our day. Where are we in relation to the monthly bills? The annual budget and property taxes? Is it too late in my life to switch careers, try a new hobby? Can this old dog really learn a new trick? This time-centric focus can be the cause for a great deal of stress,and it's all conditioned by our experience.

Not everyone shares the same values about time as those in the modern West. Perhaps you've heard of the "island mentality": We'll get to it when we get to it, they say.

What freedom! When I first moved to Los Angeles from Minnesota, I was struck by the comparatively laid-back approach to scheduling that Angelenos embraced. In particular, it seemed like no one was in any sort of rush to return phone calls. My take on it is that, in a land of endless summer, there really is the feeling of more time available to do the things we want to do. In Minnesota, there are seasons to contend with: you better enjoy these long days of summer while you can! The brutal winter with 60-below temps is just a few months away.

And while Los Angeles seemed like "island mentality" to a Minnesotan like me, I experienced true island thinking when I went to Maui.

This is a tiny island! It takes three hours to drive the entire length, sometimes going 10 mph due to one-lane sections of road. Nowhere to go, nowhere to be. Just takin' it slow.

We are taught our way of thinking about—and valuing—time, along with many other values handed down to us. What values do you cling to that cause you unnecessary stress? We'll dig more deeply into your value system a bit later.

What to Make of It All

As you can see, we've picked up a lot of preconditioning in how we handle stress—in some areas, millions of years of predisposition, but that doesn't mean we have to let stress continue to rule us. We owe it to ourselves and everyone around us to interrupt these old tendencies and live our lives with less stress.

What does less stress mean for us? We've lived with it for this long—why not just keep swimming, even if it feels like it's always upstream? Change is difficult. It's easier to just stay the same, right?

Observing the effects of chronic stress, which we'll do in the next chapter, will highlight the importance—the urgency, even—of taking a proactive stance towards decreasing our levels of stress. Our "live-ly-hood" depends on it!

▌ Activity—See Through Your Stress

Which one of the following foundations of being causes you the most stress?

- Identification with Self vs. "other"

- Resistance to change

- Pursuit of pleasure, avoidance of pain

- Your past conditioning

The ways we respond to situations—especially stressful ones—have evolved to keep us safe. Hyper-vigilance helps the young child in us see, in advance, danger lurking.   In what ways has the stressor you chose above served you? Has it kept you safe? Has it developed into a keen sense of human nature? Of the world?

In what ways do these feelings of stress prevent your happiness now?

When we recognize that our ways of being came about as a positive adaptation to our environment, and know that we can lovingly release those ways that now hold us back, we find a willingness to work through the stress that causes us pain. Through this opening, we can invite a less constrictive way of living to take hold.

Answer the above questions in your journal, and choose which of these stressful responses you can stop doing today. It only takes one decision applied over the next 30 days to bring about a profound shift towards more freedom.

Adam Timm

Chapter Four

Pain is a relatively objective, physical phenomenon; suffering
is our psychological resistance to what happens. Events may
create physical pain, but they do not in themselves create
suffering. Resistance creates suffering.

Stress happens when your mind resists what is . . .
The only problem in your life is your mind's
resistance to life as it unfolds."
—Dan Millman

▌ Feeling the Effects of Chronic Stress

The body is amazing, working in so many ways of perfection, and allowing us to experience all that life offers—to taste delicious foods, to smell fantastic fragrances, and feel the vast array of emotions that move through us in the course of a day—and the stress response is borne of the same perfection.

In the course of protecting us from danger, the stress response works perfectly. When we need a spike of energy before we get on stage, it's there to help us rise to our best.

We evolved to handle these bursts of stress. They come and go without being unnatural, just a part of the terrific tapestry of life. However, we lose when ongoing, mild to moderate stresspushes us around, day-in and day-out.

There are many of us who are getting pushed around by chronic stress. According to the 2000 "Attitudes In The American Workplace IV" Gallup poll, 80 percent of employees suffer from workplace stress, with nearly 40 percent reporting they need help in managing their stress. Many studies suggest that stress is a contributing factor in the development of chronic and degenerative conditions, such as heart disease and diabetes. High stress levels at work also lead to job burnout, reduction in productivity, ill health, job dissatisfaction, absenteeism, and increased turnover.

Job stress costs American businesses hundreds of billions of dollars per year.

Sixty percent of all absences are due to stress-related issues, costing employers more than $57 Billion a year.

Workers reporting themselves as "stressed" incur health care costs that are 46 percent higher than other employees.[7]

Physical Effects of Chronic Stress

We know that stress hurts. We know it costs us money. But what really happens to our bodies when the stress response kicks in?

Imagine it's 10,000 BC, and you're leading your tribe through treacherous terrain, constantly scanning the horizon for threats, all senses piqued by the possibility of danger. Suddenly a saber-toothed tiger leaps from behind a rock and takes chase.

In an instant, your pituitary gland signals the adrenal glands to flood your bloodstream with stress hormones, including adrenaline and cortisol. Your heart rate increases, more oxygen flows throughout the body, and your senses heighten further as blood is directed away from digestion and other non-essential functions.

Your immune system is suppressed to free up resources. You can run faster, perform with more strength, think more quickly, respond through instinct, and feel less pain—all because of this natural response to imminent danger.

After a heroic battle, you and your fellow warriors are able to drive the saber-toothed tiger away, setting up camp not much farther down the path. After cooling down and relaxing a bit, the levels of adrenaline and cortisol in your system decrease, bringing down your heart rate, and bringing back online all the other normal functions of the body. This is how our bodies are designed to handle stress:

EVENT → RESPONSE → ACTION (fight or flee) → COOLDOWN

ALL SYSTEMS BACK TO NORMAL

Some funny things start to happen when the body endures ongoing bouts of chronic stress with no opportunity to recover, however.

In a tragic twist, the same system that helps us to rise to our best during the most difficult times begins to eat away at the body's good health like salt and rust eat away the undercarriage of a car in the Minnesota winter.

Without unplugging from the continual onslaught of stress hormones, our bodies eventually break down. Exactly where the blowout occurs depends on the person, but the many systems affected by chronic stress mean there are ample chances for burnout.

Cardiovascular System

We'll start with the "heart" of the matter. The main components of the cardiovascular system include the heart, blood, and blood vessels. Every minute your heart circulates the entire contents of your body's blood (about 5 quarts), bringing oxygen from the tips of your toes to the point of your nose.

Over the course of our lives, this circulation can become more difficult for the heart, as blood vessels become constricted (due to plaque build-up) or as there is more tissue for the blood to circulate through (due to obesity). As the heart pumps harder and faster, heart rate and blood pressure increase. Add some stress to the mix and you've got an even quicker heart rate, and even more pressure. Things start to get tense—literally (hypertension!).

An increased heart rate in the heat of battle is one thing, but when it isn't allowed to return to normal because of continuous, low-grade to moderate stress, we are put at risk of heart attack and stroke.

Most heart attacks and strokes are the result of an arterial blockage caused when there is a rupture inside of an artery, causing a blood clot to form (just like when we have a cut on our finger). As this clot moves through the bloodstream, getting hung up on plaques along the arterial wall, it limits the flow of blood to the heart or brain. The probability of a rupture is greatly increased when we have chronically high blood pressure. In fact, high blood pressure is the most important modifiable risk factor of stroke.[8]

Even if you haven't been diagnosed with a heart condition, the importance of limiting episodes of high blood pressure and preventing hypertension is evident when we look at how widespread heart disease really is. Coronary artery disease (CAD; also known as atherosclerotic heart disease) is the result of the accumulation of atheromatous plaques within the walls of the coronary arteries.[9] This accumulation starts in childhood, and it is accelerated by factors like genetics, diet, level of exercise.

Most people with CAD won't show symptoms for decades, until the advanced stages of the disease cause a "sudden" heart attack. This disease is the most common cause of sudden death,[10] and is also the most common reason for death in men and women over 20 years of age.[11]

According to present trends in the United States, half of healthy 40-year-old males will develop coronary artery disease in the future, as will one in three healthy 40-year-old women.[12]

These are huge numbers, but we can greatly reduce the risk of heart attack and death as the result of heart disease by doing something about our stress levels. How motivated are you? It's one thing to understand intellectually what's going on, it's another to take action. When we decrease stress, our blood pressure decreases, and we increase our chances of joyful living.

While taking action is essential, it can be hard to do anything when we feel so run down. It doesn't help that chronic hit the digestive system just as hard as the cardiovascualar system.

| Digestive System

The digestive system includes, in order of appearance, the mouth, esophagus, stomach, small intestine (which is linked to the pancreas, liver, and gall bladder), and the large intestine (which includes the colon, rectum, and anus).

> When that rush of stress hormones hits our digestive system, the release of stomach acid is slowed, and the emptying of the stomach is put on hold. There's no need to digest food when we're about to take evasive action.

These same hormones, cortisol and adrenaline, stimulate the colon as well, speeding the passage of its contents. When we're particularly stressed, like when suddenly scared or afraid, we might completely lose control of our bowels. I'm sure you've heard the saying "scared shitless."

In short bursts, this process works beautifully. Suppressing the digestive process leaves us more energy for the high-alert situation in front of us and focuses the body's attention. After the threat has passed and stress hormones have dissolved, digestion resumes as usual. But in a chronic stress scenario, the functional goodness of the stress response is overridden, ushering in symptoms that aren't so good.

These uncomfortable symptoms include constipation, acid indigestion, and even ulcers. Maybe you know someone who is highly anxious and regularly complains of stomachaches. That someone was me not too long ago. In the midst of work stress, relationship stress, and a general feeling of discontentment with life, I would wake up with intensely painful indigestion, guzzle some Pepto and try to go back to sleep.

At the time, I didn't put two-and-two together. I just went to the doctor and was prescribed some medical-grade antacid. Not exactly a solution, per se, but it helped with the symptom. Several trips back to the physician, and I was still being told the same thing: "No ulcer, but take these tablets and the symptoms should decrease. Come back if they don't."

> It wasn't until I rooted out the factors of my life that were causing stress that I found lasting relief from my symptoms, *without medication.*

The problem with addressing just the symptom, as opposed to the underlying cause, was that the symptoms kept coming up any time I stopped taking the medication. It wasn't until I rooted out the factors of my life that were causing stress that I found lasting relief from my symptoms, without medication.

Not only does chronic stress inhibit the body's digestive process and produce these nasty symptoms, but the nutrition from the food that we do eat doesn't get absorbed properly by our agitated lower intestine. So there we are, stressed out and feeling low, and the body can't get the very nutrients it needs to get out of this funk. This lack of sustenance puts our good health at risk, especially combined with another aspect of chronic stress—our compromised immune system.

Immune System

The immune system is made up of the cells and functions that protect our bodies from pathogens that might cause us illness. Looking back at that saber-toothed tiger attack—in an effort to save the body's energy for the fight-or-flight response, the stress hormone cortisol suppresses the regular functioning of the immune system.

By now, you know the drill: for a short amount of time, all good, no problem. But chronically, day-in and day-out, an out-of-whack immune system leaves our bodies exposed to invaders. When this happens, colds and other infections can easily take over.

Much research has shown the negative effect stress has on the immune system, mostly through studies where participants were subjected to a variety of viruses. In one study, individuals caring for a spouse with dementia, representing the stressed group, saw a significant decrease in immune response when given an influenza-virus vaccine compared to a non-stressed control group.[13]

> In an effort to save the body's energy for the fight-or-flight response, the stress hormone cortisol suppresses the regular functioning of the immune system.

A similar study was conducted using a respiratory virus. Participants were infected with the virus and given a stress index. Results showed that an increase in score on the stress index correlated with greater severity of cold symptoms.[14]

The higher the stress level, the sicker we get. The last thing we want to do when we feel anxious and tense is get sick, but it so easily happens. Our health and livelihood is further impacted by the way chronic stress impacts the endocrine system.

Endocrine System

The endocrine system is the system of glands that secrete hormones into the bloodstream to regulate various aspects of the body. These hormones regulate metabolism, water balance, bone development, blood sugar levels, estrogen levels in women, and testosterone levels in men. Specific to the hormones that regulate our libido, estrogen and testosterone, a stressful event shuts off our desire for sex—no reason to fornicate when the only option is to fight or flee. Chronic stress dampens our sex drive on a more permanent basis. In women, chronic stress increases the severity of PMS symptoms.

These factors can be difficult when it comes to our personal relationships, especially when we would benefit from the support offered by these relationships. Unfortunately we only manage to push people farther away because of the stress we feel.

Central Nervous System

The central nervous system is the nexus of the stress response—where it all goes down. This system includes the combination of the brain, the spinal cord, and all of the nerves that flow out of the spinal cord. This is yet another area where the momentary burst of stress—in that moment when we need to mobilize—causes the body to respond instinctively and mitigate the threat in our environment.

Cortisol and adrenaline are released, producing the effects described above, all in an effort to prepare the body to fight or flee. The production of serotonin, a neurotransmitter that regulates mood and digestion, is decreased.

Cortisol sensitizes and stimulates the amygdala (the alarm bell in the brain), so it becomes ever more reactive to stress, stimulating more cortisol production.

The body is readied, action is taken. We survive the threat, and the response passes, except when we're trapped in the cycle of chronic stress. In this case, the ongoing onslaught of cortisol wears on areas of the brain, creating a vicious cycle.

This vicious cycle begins with ongoing doses of cortisol (the result of the continual perception of a threat on our lives) flooding the system. Cortisol sensitizes and stimulates the amygdala (the alarm bell in the brain), so it becomes ever more reactive to stress, stimulating more cortisol production.

Chronic production of cortisol then weakens the hippocampus. The hippocampus is the area of the brain that forms memory from context and also helps to quiet the amygdala. In extreme cases, chronic stress-related cortisol levels can shrink the hippocampus by up to 25 percent.

The result is that the alarm bell warning of an impending stressful event is getting louder and louder, but the body's ability to turn the volume down gets weaker and weaker. We become ever more reactive to stress, creating more stress in the future, in a grim downward spiral.[15]

Coupled with the decrease in serotonin production (serotonin regulates our mood: less serotonin, less happy), this cycle truly drags us into the proverbial mud of life, sometimes making it hard to "keep our heads up," as we're always told to do. The body is effectively conditioned to behave in this way, exacerbating the situation with each new bout of stress, which hits us harder every time.

After years of this, it's no wonder that our view of the world is simply: "Stressed-out". Everywhere we look in our lives, there's another example of tension and claustrophobia. Our personal relationships, our work situation, our lack of free time, the commute to work—they all point back to that familiar and nagging feeling that things are not right, which bring us more stress.

General Pain and Discomfort

Aside from the various systems of the body being affected in the specific ways listed above, chronic stress brings about all sorts of aches and pains that eventually become a part of our everyday life, sapping our energy in ways that we possibly aren't even aware of. A few of them are:

- Anxiety
- Back Pain
- Constipation
- Depression
- Fatigue
- Weight gain or loss

- Insomnia
- Relationship problems
- Shortness of breath
- Stiff neck
- Upset stomach
- Diarrhea

When we live with these symptoms day-in and day-out, we start to think this is just how it is.

> We define ourselves as someone who is anxious, or as someone who has a sore back and stiff neck, or someone who is always tired and depressed. We wrongly associate who we are with the symptoms of our stressful life.

When we do this, something is lost. We lose faith in ourselves. We become even more stressed. We go to the doctor again and again, searching for a cure, when there really isn't anything wrong, except that we need to approach our lives from a fresh perspective.

Instead of seeing symptoms of stress and resigning ourselves to the idea that this is all there is, we can look at our lives, see where we are experiencing daily stress, and then see the symptoms for what they are.

> We aren't suffering from some strange disease in need of a miracle cure; we just need to unplug from the sources of stress in our lives so that the body can return to its normal resting state.
> When we stop stressing, the body can take care of the rest.

The symptoms we experience are really just signposts, pointing our focus in the direction of where there's a problem. Once we locate the problem, we can do something about it. *With awareness comes the power to take action.*

Lifestyle Choices That Add to the Body's Stress Level

Aside from the body's natural reaction to stress, conditioned by the way we think, there are certain ways of living that increase the body's susceptibility to becoming overstressed.

What We Eat/How We Eat—Nutrition

Many of us do not receive the nutrients we need to stay healthy, active, and alert. We don't eat enough vegetables. We eat too much processed food, high in sugar, saturated fats, and sodium, and it lacks the basic building blocks that keep us going strong, complex carbohydrates, high-quality protein, good fats, and micronutrients (vitamins and minerals).

In addition to this, we often eat out of an emotional need to calm our stressful thoughts. We eat the kind of comfort food that we're used to, which ususally isn't the best for our bodies. The vicious cycle continues: We get stressed, and we eat because we're stressed, causing us to feel more stressed when we come down from the sugar high, which makes us keep eating.

Begin to pay close attention to how you eat. Are you eating lots of fresh vegetables? Are you eating a diet low in unhealthy fats? Do you frequently eat junk food because you're stressed?

See if you can cut back the amount of processed foods you eat, and consider your reasons for eating the way you do.

Level of Activity—Exercise

When we are stressed, in addition to eating poorly, we are more likely to forgo regular exercise, which leaves the body more vulnerable to stress. The body needs exercise to stay at its optimal level. To stay healthy and feeling good, we need at least a minimal amount of daily exercise. Without it, the body stops functioning correctly:We get tired easily. We succumb to the habits of eating poorly to keep our energy levels boosted..

How much exercise are you getting? Can you begin getting more today? Even taking the stairs instead of the elevator can make a difference.

With proper nutrition and enough exercise, we boost the body's natural defenses, and help prevent the onset of the mental effects of stress, which are detailed in the next chapter.

Activity—See Through Your Stress

When we unplug from the stress in our lives, the body's natural systems are allowed to regulate themselves in a healthy way.

Use the following exercises to decrease your feelings of stress anytime:

- Take three deep breaths, exhaling deeply, feeling the tension drain from your neck, back, and shoulders. Feel your feet on the ground, the chair beneath you. Notice how you are supported. Consciously allow yourself to relax.

- Whenever you can, call to mind a feeling of safety, of being around good people, of something that brings you joy.

- If you're dealing with something particularly stressful today, see if you can breathe into it, allowing the stressful thoughts just to linger in your mind as you bring your attention to the feelings and sensations of the breath. Notice how, as you bring your attention to the breath, the stressful feelings fade. Continue for as long as you'd like.

The more often you use these exercises, the more your body will become accustomed to "unplugging" from the stress response. With regular practice, things will get much easier.

One of the most powerful practices that I know of to combat stress and create more space in your day is "The Breath of Freedom."

For a guided example of how to use "The Breath of Freedom," follow this link:

http://www.liveazenlife.com/breathoffreedom

Chapter Five

"If your teeth are clenched and your fists are clenched, your lifespan is probably clenched."
—Adabella Radici

Mental Effects of Chronic Stress

As we've seen, when exposed to chronic bouts of daily stress and the hormones released from them, the body's systems become locked in the perpetual grip of the stress response, never allowing it to regain a state of rest. When the body's systems can't relax, we feel it.

Have you ever tried to sit still on your day off and found it nearly impossible? The only thing that you can do is think about the next thing you have to do. Or maybe you just sit there, feeling anxious, or feeling any of the many other pains that stress brings about for you.

The physical symptoms of chronic stress, along with that sinking feeling we're so familiar with, bring up all kinds of persuasive thought patterns, and they're not usually positive. We play the victim, throw temper tantrums, and get into frequent arguments, all because we're over it. We're tired of feeling tired all the time. But not all kind of stress are necessarily harmful.

Going back to what was said earlier about acute stress (Remember? The kind that makes championship teams?), there is a striking difference between how our minds are affected by short bursts of acute stress compared to chronic stress. With a bout of acute stress—say, right before you get on stage for your cheer team routine in the finals—the rush of stress hormones focuses the mind and brings clarity in the midst of this big moment. Sure, the nerves are there, and there may be a bit of fear, but once you get on stage, it all clicks. All the practice pays off. You nail each twist, each pose, every fist-pump, and the team snaps together for the win.

Stress tunes us up in these moments, allowing us to rise to the occasion. Then the euphoria wears off, our bodies unwind, and the stress hormones dissipate. Life goes back to normal. Our thoughts return to whatever is in front of us.

But chronic stress and the thoughts it provokes are a bit less inspiring. There's no rush of excitement for what's to come, no feelings of accomplishment to look forward to—just another stressed-out day. Even if we're not aware that we are surrounded by chronic stress, our mindset points it out. We might experience hopelessness, thoughts or feelings of disconnection, or condescending or negative thoughts about aspects of our surroundings and the situation before us. We might express this negativity by using sarcasm or having a short fuse with the people in our lives. There might be an ever-present feeling that something is wrong, but we can never really put our finger on it.

Our hobbies no longer distract us enough to make this static of discontent go away. Our relationships no longer provide with us the comfort they once did. Our work doesn't satisfy. Our bosses are nags. Our side projects never turn into what we had hoped for—and there may have been many that showed great promise.

We can't decide what to do or where to go. But we know HERE is NOT where it's at. There is no freedom living like this.

❚ Action as an Avoidance Mechanism

And so we self-medicate: We change mates, move somewhere new, pursue an untried endeavor, try an exotic restaurant, have a drink, go on a trip, watch some more TV, spend quality time with our spouse (or that hot new someone). We do everything we can think of to make this feeling, these thoughts, go away. As we rearrange the deck chairs on the sinking ship that is our life, changing only the external factors of a problem that is deeply rooted in the very way we think through life, we grow more tired, more stressed. This is what being stuck on the hamster wheel is all about.

That's not to say that our self-medication doesn't bring us moments of joy. Moving to a new home, starting a new job, and getting a new girlfriend or boyfriend all bring some sort of excitement in their newness, right? It's fresh, never been tasted, the greener grass that we were hoping for. But after the newness wears off we're left with a familiar feeling. That dull ache of tension and exhaustion comes throbbing from beneath our newfound happiness—or what we thought was happiness—causing thoughts and feelings similar to those we were sure we had left behind.

> As we rearrange the deck chairs on the sinking ship that is our life, changing only the external factors of a problem that is deeply rooted in the very way we think through life, we grow more tired, more stressed.

We might not recognize them as the same thoughts that drove us to these greener pastures, however. Now that we have different external circumstances, we blame those circumstances instead. For example, you move. The old place was in a rundown neighborhood, and the new place is managed by slumlords and surrounded by picky neighbors. The old job offered too little pay for too much work, and now your current job—for a lot more money—forces you to deal with rude and insensitive people all day long. The old girlfriend was boring, but the new girlfriend is crazy. After enough of these cycles, we might finally arrive at rock bottom. "No matter what I do, it's the same!" we exclaim, defeated.

The problem isn't the external circumstances. The problem is our avoidance of dealing with the stress that is pushing us around. And when the bright and shiny paint on our new circumstances gets scuffed, dulling the distraction that newness often provides, the truth resurfaces. We are still stressed

> "No matter what I do, it's the same!" we exclaim, defeated.

out, maybe even more stressed now that our new stuff has failed to bring us lasting joy. This is coupled with the fact that chronic stress invariably taints our view of the world, making us much more prone to thinking that the glass is half-empty. When we are busy getting used to new circumstances, we forget what's lurking beneath the surface. We forget what we are running from in the first place.

Inaction as an Avoidance Mechanism

Or on the other hand, maybe we don't change anything. We don't run. We just remain in that stuck place, caught between the stress and the circumstances we think might be causing it. Maybe we're too tired, too full of fear, too beaten down to change anything, even though something *must* change.

This life is not what you signed up for. You plop yourself in front of the TV and disconnect from life. Shovel another few donuts in your mouth. "Mmm, they taste so good, even though I shouldn't..." We put off that much-needed change—whatever it is—for another day. When? Who cares, I'm watching my favorite show.

> Chronic stress invariably taints our view of the world, making us much more prone to thinking the glass is half-empty.

In this situation, instead of being driven to changethings in an attempt to feel better, we attempt to rest in the comfort of our old habits: Eating comfort food,feeling sorry for ourselves, and blaming others for the less-than-inspiring life that we've created. And while it might feel okay for now to drown ourselves in donuts and self-pity, this feeling passes quite quickly as reality comes back around.

With enough of these trips between avoidance and stark reality,, we experience whiplash.. We know on some level that we have to change something other than just the channel, or the kind of dessert we're choosing. We need something deep, something lasting.

The Truth

The bitter truth is that we gravitate towards short-term fixes for these stress-induced thought patterns that have taken years, maybe our entire lifetime, to develop. The "fixes" are a manifestation of the discontent brought about by the stress we feel. I'm sure you've heard of the law of attraction, the law which posits, "Like attracts like." It can be further explained as the fact that you are much more likely to draw into your life those things that you are most closely resonating with. Maybe you've heard someone say that the people in your life are a reflection of some aspect of you, even if you're not aware of it.

For example, for most of my 20s, I was quite discontent— Angry. Angsty. Somewhat of a jerk. During this season of discontent, I broke up with a long-term girlfriend (we'll call her Amanda) and hopped right into another relationship (with Sharon, we'll say). The relationship with Sharon also became long-term. As the years went by, it became clear that I had drawn in a partner just as discontented as I was. As the newness (the honeymoon stage) wore off, it became less and less tolerable.

Then one day, it was luminously clear to me that the relationship was no longer in alignment with what I was feeling. I was no longer outwardly discontented with the world, and this relationship was a holdover from my past. I needed to make a change and bring the external circumstances of my life into alignment with my growing sense of internal joy and contentment. We ended it. Had we stayed together any longer after coming to this realization, we would only have prolonged our unhappiness.

When we gravitate towards quick fixes and short-term solutions to problems that require a fundamental shift in the way we approach life, more stress and more discontentment is the result.

❚ The Mind and Stress

The body, under fire from a constant onslaught of stress hormones, is shaken-up, off-kilter, and trying desperately to regain its balance. The reflexive thoughts that arise in this state attempt to direct us to this equilibrium. But when we are constantly on alert, fear and doubt cloud these thoughts, shade our judgment, and leave us less prepared to make sound choices. We can't see straight.

This entire process of becoming stressed starts with a mental perception of a threat. It might not be on the level of our conscious awareness, but it's there, lingering, hanging out when we encounter a situation that has proved stressful in the past.

Traffic is again a great example. Depending on our relationship with our morning commute, we can start to become tense at the thought of the traffic that awaits us even as we're getting ready in the morning. It's a subtle, maybe imperceptible tension. Then, when we know that our fears have been realized (as we come to a complete stop after traffic seemed to be happily moving along at 60 mph), the tension enter our conscious awareness. It surrounds us. It clouds our view of that person in front of us. "Why is he braking?!" To the person alongside us: "Don't you dare cut me off!" And on it goes.

It started way before we knew it. In fact, the stress may have never left our mind from the previous morning's commute. We kept it alive as we rolled right into our annoyances at work, and then during the drive home, then again at home. So it's always there, causing us to live our lives reflexively in a state of fight or flight, as we've seen. The limbic system, when activated, takes over our bodies. The result of the stress hormones flowing to every nook and cranny is claustrophobia, and it doesn't stop there. Then we add on all the things we do to attempt to escape from the stress and tension.

When the stress response helps us make a quick escape from danger, this is natural and functional. When chronic stress invades our every moment, this is unnatural, detrimental to our health, and to the cause of mental dysfunction. Action from this state of dysfunction creates more stress. Inaction from this state of dysfunction also creates more stress.

You might be asking yourself, "What, then? Are we not supposed to take a break? Indulge in our favorite desserts? Watch TV?"

Or

"We can't change our bad circumstances? I'm just supposed to sit here?"

Conscious Change vs. Unconscious Reaction

What must be understood is that we just keep kicking the can down the road if we don't attack the root of the problem. We need a way to step outside of the stress so that we can make sound decisions and stop the stressful cycle. Action and inaction, when done out of neurotic reflex, is the problem.

When we are aware of our actions, and when they are aligned with our values and goals, then we can truly learn from them. We can be a conscious creator, instead of an unconscious interloper, in our own lives.

For millions of years, stressors in our environment have created the friction needed to direct our species into the most beneficial areas for survival and growth. These stressors, like food supply, seasonal weather changes, geological changes, predators, and a host of other factors completely out of human control, have required a reactive and automatic stance by the human body to ensure survival.

Just in the last 10,000 years have humans been in a position to decide where they wanted to go and when, but at great risk and peril. Even more recently—only in the last 80 to 100 years—have large numbers of people enjoyed the comforts of technology, free to make a life for themselves outside of the land they worked and with the large families they helped support.

Now, more than ever, we have a choice. We have the ability to use our time the way we want. Opportunities abound to live the lives we desire. In every direction we turn, there is a new avenue to pursue, if it should please us—and we can make choices that cause us more or less stress.

Why would we pursue a path of more stress? How could we let this happen? Through the confusion and discontent brought on by chronic stress, we lose sight of the things that can save us. We forget to play. We run ourselves into the ground. We see everyone around us also running around getting so much done, we feel we have to do the same—just another aspect of keeping up with the Joneses. But at what cost? We're even told or shown that if we're not stressed about the things in our life, we don't care enough.

Think about a recent argument you might have had with your spouse. In that moment where you finally surrender your standpoint—lowering your voice, relaxing your shoulders, disengaging from the battle—your spouse says, "Oh, I see, you just don't care!" Because you no longer seem stressed about what's going on, it's interpreted as detachment, complacency, or a lack of interest.

Where else in your life are you being shown that choosing a life of less stress means you don't care?

At a recent corporate training event where I spoke on stress-reducing breathing techniques, the host and I walked around the company building, inviting employees to join us. Stopping in the office of a company high-flyer (corner office, slick suit), I found his response to our invitation quite telling.

Host to high-flyer: "Would you like to participate in a session to learn some quick techniques to de-stress at your desk?"

High-flyer to host: "No thanks, I wouldn't want to lose my edge."

The message, from our home life all the way to our work life, is that the tense edge and reflexive emotion evoked by stress is the way we must be in life. If we're not overtly passionate in our personal exchanges, we don't care. If we don't remain tense and alert at work, then we don't have a competitive edge.

So many of our choices flow from implicit messages all around us. Some of these messages have been force-fed to us all our lives.

To affect lasting and powerful change, we must bring these unconsciously held beliefs into our awareness. We cannot choose to change when we aren't aware of what needs changing. The quality of our consciousness, the level of our personal awareness, determines whether we can relax into what's before us, and also change the things we must. In short, we don't know what we don't know.

It's our personal responsibility to expand our what we know about ourselves and our situation so that we can confidently see clearly. When we can see what needs changing and go for it, we move from the reactive stance of fear (stress), into a proactive stance of power.

Chronic stress prevents this "right-seeing." When we are stressed, our brains are physically prevented from working in creative ways to solve problems. Our memory is inhibited, we become anxious, and we're unable to learn from our surroundings; and we're stuck running the same old default thought patterns we always have.

One study used rats to show the effects of chronic stress on memory by exposing them to a cat for five weeks. Their stress was measured by observing their behavior in an open field as well as memory for a water maze.

In the water maze, rats were taught the location of a platform placed below the surface of the water. They had to recall this location in order to discover the platform and exit the water. It was found that the rats exposed to chronic stress could not learn to adapt to new situations and environments, and had impaired memory in the water maze.[16]

And this is no different from the way our brains work. People with Type 2 diabetes brought on by poor eating habits and lack of exercise sometimes use an insulin shot so they can maintain the same unhealthy behaviors that brought on the diabetes in the first place.

Stress leads to eating as an avoidance mechanism (comfort food) and skipping exercise (too tired to do anything). Chronically poor lifestyle habits like these lead to diabetes, and instead of looking at all of this as a sign that something must change, insulin shots are used as a method to continue living the in the same old rut. Type 2 diabetes, along with many other health maladies, is a symptom of a larger problem in thinking,

Another example of how stress can affect our way of thinking has to do with public speaking. If any of you have gotten in front of a group to give a prepared speech, you know how stressful this can be. You practice your talk a few times, get all your speaking points in order, and are feeling very confident. "I'm gonna knock this one out of the park!" you think. Visions of public speaking glory dance in your head.

And then the day of the speech comes. Butterflies isn't quite the right term for the feeling in your stomach, more like frantic bats trying to escape a collapsing cave.

You take the stage, approach the lectern to deliver this wonderful speech, and suddenly the visions of greatness turn into feelings of terror. Your brain short-circuits, leading you to bumble about nervously, eyes flitting across the room as you attempt to keep your composure. The sweat is flowing now. It sure wasn't like this when you practiced it. And then, mercifully, it's over.

"What happened up there?" you ask yourself. You may not even recall how it went or how you got up there at all. The perception of stress and, more appropriate to this situation, feelings of fear (which is stress at the body level), put the brain in autopilot, returning our behavior to a level of pre-thought.

Yes, you can function with no brain under extreme duress. In fact, the stress response to danger when you are running from a flood or a wild animal is to bypass the conscious mind because you don't need your reasoning. The brain shuts off so the body can move where it needs to go *fast* . That's why we read reports of everyday heroes who don't remember lifting a car off a child or rescuing someone from a burning building—they just do it.

In our stressed-out day-to-day life, the same thing happens to a lesser degree; we respond how we've always responded through learned behaviors and habits, not from a level of conscious thought. If we don't know how to work consciously with these feelings of stress, our default mode takes over—our default mode of fear-based non-thinking. In other words, we become zombies.

Rewiring Our Default Settings

The great news is that nothing on the level of the body (which includes all ways of thinking, being, doing) is set in stone. Once we're aware of the stress that we feel and decide to do something about it, there is a shift. With the practices that follow, you can turn this awareness into an understanding of how you relate to the stressors in your life. And from this understanding, you can take action to make chronic stress optional instead of automatic.

> If we don't know how to work consciously with these feelings of stress, default mode takes over: Our default mode of fear-based non-thinking.

These symptoms are mentioned not to induce fear, not to seed despair and sadness, but to tune your awareness to the importance of limiting the amount of stress we feel in our lives. With awareness comes hope. With hope comes the mental clarity that inspires action. We can put actions in place today to live happier lives tomorrow!

█ Activity—See Through Your Stress

Take a moment to center yourself, and bring your attention to your breath. Take three long breaths, allowing the tension to melt down through your feet and into the ground with each out-breath (use The Breath of Freedom!).

In this relaxed and centered place, reflect on the following questions:

Write down an example of a decision that you made from a stressed-out position that created future challenges.

What did you learn from this decision?

Where are you continuing to make decisions that could possibly lead to more stress?

When we see the results of decisions that flow from a stressed-out mind and understand how they sometimes lead to further discontentment, we can interrupt this habit of reaching reflexively for the next thing to save us.

Grounded reflection on major life decisions yields more confidence, more power, and greater alignment with what's going on in the larger picture of our lives.

Chapter Six

"Sometimes it's important to work for that pot of gold. But other times it's essential to take time off and to make sure that your most important decision in the day simply consists of choosing which color to slide down on the rainbow."

—Douglas Pagels

What Can We Do?

By now, you are acutely aware of what chronic stress does to the body, and hopefully you've identified some areas of your life that will benefit from decreasing your overall stress level. You may have even accepted the invitation to slow down a bit, releasing the grip of tension. This is where the path to freedom blows wide open. It's easy to see that stress is the enemy—not the things that stress us out (because these change as we change), but stress itself.

More stress = more fear, more caution, more tension. More anxiety = a slow death.

As we rush about trying to pacify this static of discontent, the stress spills over into other areas of our lives. We get drunk to quell

> It's easy to see that stress is the enemy—not the things that stress us out (because these change as we change), but stress itself.

the feeling of being stressed at work, only to have our family feel ostracized because we haven't spent quality time with them in weeks.

So many of the things we do in the interest of decreasing our stress levels are this way. They actually create more, instead of less, stress. We are like an empty vessel. We come into this world with a baseline level of stress, or a predisposition to reacting to stressful events in a certain way. As we discussed earlier, past conditioning plays a large part in our individual response to stressors.

Over time, we fill our bodies and minds with stress, slowly (or not so slowly) approaching a red line (see diagram below). When we hit our red line, something might happen. We suffer a panic attack, we experience a stroke or some other health problem, or we get into an accident because we ar-

> So many of the things we do in the interest of decreasing our stress levels are this way. They actually create more, instead of less, stress.

en't focused. To prevent this, we need to stop the accumulation of chronic stress and reverse it.

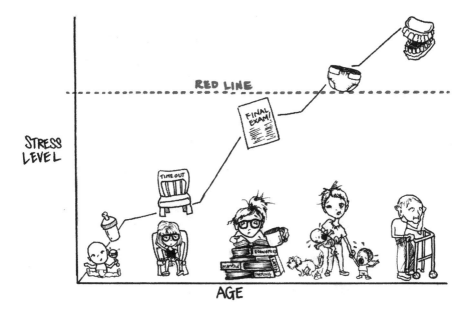

To stop the stress, we need a practice that allows us to do so. Such a practice must meet four criteria:

1. It must engage the brain at a different level than where the stress is being created.

2. Such a practice must be able to inform the rest of our life. In other words, it can't be something that we do for an hour once a week (such as going to church), and then forget about it. It must be able to soak into all the cracks of our lives in order to change us at the fundamental level.

3. This practice can't simply be a distraction from our daily stress. Watching TV, overeating, drinking heavily, smoking cigarettes, or other

4. such addictions do not reduce the overall level of stress in our system. They simply make us forget about it, suppress it, or avoid it.

5. It must be easily accessible—The easier to commit, the better.

And, of course, this practice must be done on a regular basis in order for us to feel its effects. Meditation is this practice. Along with a few other practices and exercises included later on, your relationship with stress will change forever.

Experience is what changes us. Thinking about doing something, even getting excited about the thought of doing something and then not doing it, never brings results, relief, or much of anything except a momentary good feeling.

How many of us have acted this way about some new diet, exercise regimen, or hobby? I know I have many times, but I've also seen persistence, patience, and daily practice pay off.

I'd like to share a few **success stories** with you that beautifully illustrate how we can go from stressed out and overwhelmed to feeling abundantly joyful when we commit to living a new way.

▌ DAVID

I knew David for years before he became a client. I watched in awe as he created and sold his first TV show by age 22, bringing him almost overnight success. By the time he was 26, he owned a $70,000 BMW and a $2,000,000 condo in Santa Monica, and he was parlaying his success in the entertainment industry into huge success in the real estate world. This success came easily to David; it was his natural inclination. Brash, unapologetic, and brilliant, he saw opportunity at each turn. He was inspiring and charismatic with the right people, and he was well on his way to being a multi-millionaire by age 30. A true "California story."

And then in 2008, the housing bubble burst, taking with it David's financial freedom. His leveraged position became a huge liability.

The bank foreclosed on the 30-unit apartment complex in which he and his wife had just invested. They were forced to move out of their condo in Santa Monica (for which they had taken on a second mortgage to finance the apartment complex), and they were left bankrupt and homeless.

They retreated back east, to Georgia, to be closer to family and to contemplate their next steps. David decided to take a consulting gig down in Costa Rica. Relaxing on the beach, he finally found peace, after seeing all that he worked for so quickly taken away. But the questions still raced in his mind. How could this happen? What should I do next? When's the next failure going to happen? These considerations became much more consuming with the birth of his first son—He needed stability to provide for his young family.

It was at about this time that David came to me. He had returned to California broke and looking for work, with his family waiting for him in Georgia. He had tried working a few jobs here and there since things went bust, but fear kept him from succeeding in these new endeavors. He would remember with fondness his earlier successes, recalling how easy it was for him to make instinctual decisions that quickly turned to gold. Now, with the specter of failure always looming in his mind, everything he touched quickly shriveled.

His was a question of confidence, of seeing beyond the fear of the past and boldly rooting himself in the present. In the present he could create the future of his dreams. The chronic stress caused by his inability to provide for his family provoked perpetual feelings of fear and doubt, which in turn caused David to gravitate towards uninspiring work to pay the bills. Without inspiration, he could not be successful, and so the cycle went.

My work with David began by bringing to his awareness the power of his experience. In his mind, full of stress (stemming from a perceived inability to provide for his own basic needs), the story of his life was one of failure. His meteoric rise and subsequent fall, to him, were an indication that it could happen again. And so he lived amidst this fearful uncertainty.

Instead of trying to convince him otherwise, I asked him to look back on his life and make a list of all of the experiences, thoughts, and actions that served him well, for which he was truly grateful. On a separate list, I asked him to make a list of those ways of thinking, acting, and being that no longer served him, which he was ready release lovingly.

Something inspiring happened to David during this exercise. He realized that many of his past failures, rather than providing only a basis for fear and doubt, were actually the launching point for much of his self-confidence, and that he was grateful for their occurrence; grateful for those experiences that, before this exercise, caused him to fear his ability to provide for his family! What a transformation!

> It was the rampant thoughts about past failures that caused David's baseline of worry and fear.

I also asked David to commit to a daily practice of sitting quietly for ten minutes each day, simply watching his breathing, stilling the mind, and allowing for a break in the thoughts that propelled him forward. It was the rampant thoughts about past failures that caused David's baseline of worry and fear.

A daily practice of meditation, of training the mind to relax, allows these thoughts, which are so compelling at times, to simply drift by without us having to act. By disrupting his stream of thoughts David was able to move beyond the old fear-based pattern of his thinking and stop it from continuing.

Within a month, David had developed another multi-million-dollar idea that he had the confidence to shop around, and he was given the opportunity to produce another TV show, this time in Miami Beach.

David saw that he could no longer live in fear. He had a vision for a different life, and the confidence to ask for assistance. His awareness of the problem and subsequent understanding of how it was keeping him in the negative feedback loop gave him the ability to act. He chose action, stuck with it daily, and returned to his former greatness with a newfound an appreciation for his vast wealth of experience.

▌ JULIA

Julia is a single mom who came to me after taking a medical leave from her job as the office manager for a private school. She cared passionately about her work, felt a strong connection with the parents of the children who attended the school, and had a vested interest in the school's success because her daughters, ages eight and ten, also went there. The school was her life.

Through this emotional attachment and tireless commitment to her work, Julia took on more and more stress. She wasn't sleeping well and had constant headaches, all from working too much. She was miserable, and her problems had been increasing over the previous six months. She had little time for her friends or her family. She had lost her sense of direction and purpose.

When she realized she couldn't remember the last time she had truly laughed and played with her children, she knew she needed to make some drastic changes.

A self-described Type-A personality, Julia felt a tremendous amount of anxiety over taking leave from her job, in addition to the fear of not having enough money to support herself and her children.

In fact, the buildup of her stress resulted in a worldview dominated by fear.

Her friends and family compounded this fear by voicing their doubts over Julia's decision to step away from her stressful workplace. A traditional Chinese family, Julia's parents and siblings had much more conservative views on she should handle her situation, and this only reinforced her fears.

It was Julia's awareness that something had to change that led her to find me. Through our work together, which included weekly coaching sessions and a daily meditation practice, she began seeing almost immediate results.

Her words:

"I had a decent night's sleep after the very first group meditation session. I work up the next morning feeling refreshed for the first time in months! I was shocked and knew this was a life-changer. I decided to begin working with Adam as a private client.

Within only two weeks, I started seeing major changes in my attitude and the way I handled stress. It was like a whole new me. I couldn't believe how easy and practical it was! Even my family noticed that I was, as they described it, my "happy self" again and that my kids were happy, too!

By the end of our six weeks of work together, I knew I had found a way to deal with any stress that came up. I feel stronger and able to face any situation. I've found myself again. Stress was literally sucking my sense of purpose, and now, after learning how to meditate and realizing how it helps every area of my life, I've been given a fresh start.

I no longer have the headaches, no longer worry about work; my kids are much happier, and I have a saner perspective on things. I'm once again excited about my future. It's difficult to put into words how amazing my life has become."

How did Julia go from being a self-professed Type Apersonality, completely stressed out with no time for herself or her kids, to being open and flowy, willing to let her life unfold in its natural course?

With Julia's awareness of how stress was stealing her happiness and tainting her time with her kids, she sought to understand how her life could be different. She took conscious action and found a solution. No longer dominated by stress-induced fear and anxiety, she was able to rekindle her passion for screenwriting and now has no plans to return to her former job. She went from fear to power and passion.

Evolve Your Personality

Psychologists have long believed that major personality make-overs are impossible. In fact, the big themes of personality (being shy or outgoing, relaxed or worried) seem to be scripted at a very young age. Recently, however, personality researchers have begun looking more closely at the smaller ways we can and do change.

Positive psychologists, who investigate human talents, have identified twenty-four character strengths—familiar qualities we admire, such as integrity, loyalty, kindness, and vitality—and are examining them to find out why these faculties come so naturally to some people. They're discovering that many of these qualities amount to habitual ways of responding to the world—habits that can be learned.[17]

Just as we can learn habits that benefit us, like working out regularly to lose weight, we can unlearn habits that we'd rather not live with, such as the stressful way we respond to certain things in our lives.

We all have within us the dynamic ability to change any single aspect of our personality, going from regularly annoyed to peacefully content; from depressingly pessimistic to expressively joyful; from high-strung to low-key.

Based on this research, it's clear we're not just who we are, and that's that. How many times have you heard this in an argument—"That's just who I am!" The truth is that we can be whatever we want to be. And in fact, we have a responsibility to change our ways of being if they cause us hardship— for ourselves and for those around us. These changes, while showing up as more positive ways of acting, being, and doing, also createfundamental changes in the way our brains work. When we change the way we relate to our world, we physically change the way our brains are wired!

Using technology called functional magnetic resonance imaging(MRI) neuroscientists discovered that the brain was not immutable after early childhood, as previously believed, but could change structurally and functionally over time in response to environmental stimulation and mental processing. The brain was not fixed but malleable.[18]

> Instead of being stuck with the same old ways of thinking that bring about the same worn-out way of stressed-out living, we can change. We can change our thoughts and actions by using specific practices to change our brains.

On the physical level, neural pathways cause our habitual ways of thinking. Whenever you meet bumper-to-bumper traffic, you experience the same cascade of emotions (dread, hopelessness, anger, tension) because your brain is following the same path each time.

It's the same with any recurring thought: Painful memories often surface in similar ways. You are reminded of a memory by something in your immediate field of

The present moment becomes entangled with the old painful memory-- tainted by this worn-out way of thinking.

awareness. You dredge up the painful memory from the depths and then ruminate on it for a while, until finally it passes, or you direct your attention to something else.

For as long as you've been bringing that old painful memory up, it has followed the same neural pathway, dragging with it all the hurt feelings and thoughts of inadequacy that were always associated with it. The present moment becomes entangled with the old painful memory—tainted by this worn way of thinking.   Chronic stress is like this old painful memory that keeps coming up. We are conditioned by years of living a certain way, years of practice. The way our brain processes signals from our environment is a lot like the way water flows over land. Over many years, the water slowly cuts into the earth, creating a canyon—a worn pathway.

But we can change these pathways; life can be what we want it to be; we can live without the stress that this worn-out pathway of thinking has brought us.

▌ The Opportunity

Just as David and Julia did, you can interrupt this stream disrupt your ordinary way of thinking, and live with less stress.

▌ Activity—See Through Your Stress

Honoring Your Experience

Pull out a fresh sheet of paper.

Find a quiet place where you can write. Take a moment to connect with your breath, relax your shoulders, feel your feet on the ground, and allow your mind to be calm.

On this sheet of paper, write down the experiences in your life that you would call failures, any recurring negative self-talk ("I'm not worthy of love," "I wish I hadn't said that," "Why am I so ugly," etc.), and any other actions that you might regret. These are the things that no longer serve you..

On a second sheet of paper, write down all of the things about your life that you are proud of. List your accomplishments, your personal compliments, and what makes you feel good about yourself. Allow the joy to flow and a smile to come over your face.

Now compare the lists. Maybe you see that some of the "failures" are actually sources of pride, tests that you have passed.

Once you are done scanning each list, take the list of thoughts, memories, and deeds that no longer serve you and plan a ceremony to release these old thoughts. You can burn this piece of paper, bury it, tear it up into little pieces—whatever feels right to you. As you do this, say, "I lovingly release that which no longer serves me."

Every challenge in your life has led you to this current moment where there is only opportunity. Each negative thought loop can be interrupted and rewiredt. If any thought of the past is no longer adding to your joy, you now have the power to release it.

Chapter Seven

~A Brief Visioning Intermission~

"Tension is who you think you should be.
Relaxation is who you are."
—Chinese Proverb

▌Understanding a New Way of Being

In order to apply practices that can help us break out of our worn patterns of thinking and make daily chronic stress a thing of the past, we must first craft a vision of a less stressful future. Once we conceive of this brighter tomorrow, we can move towards it.

▌The Reality of Today

At this point, you are probably much more aware of the stress that is a part of your everyday life. We've already asked ourselves a few tough questions about the stresses we feel, and how we might be creating more stress in our lives.

Take a moment now to reflect on the feeling of this stress.

Does it arise as subtle anxiety? Are you met with regular panic attacks?

Do you suffer from constant headaches? Upper neck and back tension? High blood pressure?

Has the doctor told you that stress is taking a toll on your health? Do you already know?

Do you feel like you have no purpose in life? That you are just "doing time" until retirement?

Do you have a short fuse? Are you constantly annoyed? Regularly pessimistic?

Do you feel like you have no time for yourself? And even if you get time for yourself, you can't enjoy it?   Okay. That's enough of that. Now, let's turn the corner and see if we can dream up a tomorrow that looks like, feels like and means freedom to you!

The Vision for Tomorrow

There is a great saying that goes, "Pain pushes until vision pulls." The pain of chronic stress has pushed you around most of your adult life. Instead of being pushed around, constantly on the defensive, bracing yourself for the next shove, you can let the inspiration of your vision for a brighter tomorrow light your path. A clear and compelling vision has the ability to rally us to our own cause. We have the power to be our own cheerleader!

> Stress has been a compelling aspect of our lives, in some cases providing the only directionality that we've experienced. We stress about money, then go get a job that we don't like; we stress about the job that we don't like, causing our relationships at home to suffer; we try to escape the suffocating relationships at home by adopting addictions or other escapist habits—all leading to more stress. We might not even think we can turn this Titanic around.

To get the juices of inspiration flowing, let's celebrate a past success. Think back to a time, when you set out to accomplish something that, when you initially considered it, seemed out of reach. Still you went for it anyway, and you did it! It can be anything that was special to you, anything that brought you deep satisfaction and joy.

Close your eyes now, and remember this feeling of accomplishment. Remember the feeling of uncertainty at first, the resolve needed to stick to it. If it was a long road to success, marvel at your perseverance, and then the joy you felt when you reached your goal. Just sit with this joy, this feeling of knowing you did a great job. Breathe into this feeling, basking in it. Let a smile come over your face. Relax with this feeling for a few minutes. Then open your eyes.

Now that this feeling of accomplishment is fresh in your mind (you might even feel the excitement throughout your body), you know that you can do this again. You have done it before.

Your Vision for a Life with Less Stress

What would a life of less stress look like?

Get a blank sheet of paper or two (or three depending on how creative you're feeling).

Now write, in as much detail as possible, a description of what this life feels like, smells like, sounds like, tastes like, looks like. Include *as much details as possible.*

You can write a list of things. You can write a story. You can break the elements of your life into categories, Family, Work, Play, and describe how each of these areas would look. Use whatever you can to make this vision as vivid as possible.

How bright is the sun shining? What do the birds sound like? Do you have time to go to the beach? Play with your children?

How does it feel to go to work? What type of work would you do?

Describe an entire day in your less stressful life. Starting with the time you wake up (would you sleep in, get up at dawn to catch the sunrise, roll out of bed whenever you wanted?), detail everything all the way until bedtime.

As you write, allow your imagination to run wild. Put yourself in that scene.

Even mention how you might respond to someone who does something that you don't agree with. We want this to be as real as it can be, and since moving to a private island isn't the most feasible option for most of us, we will still have to interact with people who might not be happy.

Maybe in the past you would've snapped at them and tried to get in the last word, to put them in their place. But in this less stressful life, maybe you just let it go, without a second thought. Your blood pressure didn't spike, your mind didn't race with all the things you think you should've said. You happily moved on about your day.

To make it fun, use colored pens or markers or crayons; draw pictures. You can even cut pictures out of a magazine and attach them to this vision. Allow yourself to play.

Once you've finished, look it over again, and let yourself feel the joy of knowing that this can be your life. It isn't fantasy. This is a vision for what is to come.

Now put this in a safe place. Any time you need a reminder of where you are going, pull this vision sheet out and let the feeling sink in. This is the vision that will pull you to success and help you kick the habit of living stressfully.

Adam Timm

Chapter Eight

"We don't see things as they are; we see them as we are."
—Anais Nin

Taking Inventory

Before we can begin a program to change the way we relate to stress, we need to take inventory of where we are right now. Assessing our values, goals, and aspirations, and determining where we're putting our time and effort can help us understand what motivates us, and whether we are devoting our time to pursuits that enrich us. A certain amount of stress can arise simply from not honoring our deepest desires.

Values

Values are who we are—not who we would like to be, not who we think we should be, but who we are in our lives, right now. Put another way, values represent our unique and individual essence, our ultimate and most fulfilling form of expression and relation. Our values serve as a compass pointing out what it means to be true to oneself. When we honor our values on a regular and consistent basis, life is good and fulfilling.

An effective way to identify your values is to look at what you must have in your life. Beyond the physical requirements of food, shelter, and community, what must you have in your life in order to be fulfilled? Must you have a form of creative self-expression? Must you have adventure and excitement, or partnership and collaboration? Must you be moving toward a sense of accomplishment or success or be surrounded with natural beauty?

What values must you absolutely honor—or part of you dies? Values could be: authenticity (speaking your truth), self-growth, integrity, love, intimacy, family, teamwork, prosperity, or a capacity for wonder.

Take some time now to brainstorm a list of the top ten values that are important you. The chart on the following page will help. When looking at the list below, don't overthink. Just tune in and pick those values that feel right to you. Which ones really call to your heart?

Purity	Thankfulness	Mercy	Patience
Self-Discipline	Self-Love	Reverence	Peacefulness
Tact	Purposefulness	Integrity	Grace
Gratitude	Humility	Forgiveness	Responsibility
Contentment	Righteousness	Enthusiasm	Truthfulness
Faith	Challenge	Confidence	Honor
Steadfastness	Idealism	Consideration	Beauty
Helpfulness	Wisdom	Service	Trustworthiness
Perseverance	Obedience	Wonder	Caring
Balance	Orderliness	Diligence	Generosity
Peace	Creativity	Faithfulness	Devotion
Courtesy	Commitment	Joy	Moderation
Courage	Trust	Respect	Friendliness
Piety	Humor	Gentleness	Recognition
Loyalty	Love	Honesty	Justice
Modesty	Tolerance	Detachment	Compassion
Determination	Cleanliness	Acceptance	Prayerfulness
Reliability	Assertiveness	Discernment	Sacrifice
Kindness	Understanding	Self-Acceptance	Accomplishment
Family	Practicality	Accountability	Fidelity
Preservation	Accuracy	Wealth	Privacy
Adventure	Fitness	Problem Solving	Flair
Progress	Calm	Freedom	Prosperity
Friendship	Punctuality	Change	Goodness
Fun	Quality	Giving	Resourcefulness
Collaboration	Good Will	Discovery	Knowledge
Responsiveness	Communication	Competence	Power
Concern for Others	Happiness	Safety	Connection
Harmony	Helpfulness	Self-Reliance	Cooperation
Innovation	Spirituality	Leadership	Strength
Tranquility	Empathy	Endurance	Unity

Once you have your list, select your three most important, a Top-Three List of Personal Values, in order of importance to you.

1.

2.

3.

To the right of these, score your sense of satisfaction—the degree to which you are honoring each value—using a scale of zero to ten.

This exercise can be particularly revealing if you find that you are not honoring the values that are highest on your list. Rankings below 7 may indicate an area of your life where you are putting up with an intolerable situation.

Looking at the example below, there are inconsistencies between the importance of the value and level of satisfaction. ing rankings,

Value	Level of Satisfaction
1. Integrity	4
2. Freedom	8
3. Authenticity	5

If this were your top three, We might see that as a result of not living with integrity you feel a certain amount of internal tension or dissonance. In other words, stress.

We can eliminate this source of stress by bringing our actions and life's circumstances more into alignment with our values. Honoring our values is inherently fulfilling even when it is difficult. If integrity ranks high for you, you may find that there are times where you suffer discomfort in order to live in accordance with that value. The discomfort will pass, and a sense of congruency with this value will remain. There is power in this feeling of rightness within ourselves.

If you've identified areas of your life where you feel out of sync with your values, there is an opportunity for positive change. Simply by living more in alignment with your values, you can decrease your levels of stress.

Our life's goals and aspirations flow from our values. The degree to which we setaccomplishmeaningful goals as we pursue uplifting aspirations has a big impact on our level of satisfaction with life. If things seem drab and uninspiring, it could be that you have strayed from what you really want to do, from what you were meant to do.

Goals and Aspirations

Aspirations are the wind beneath our wings, the ambition that motivates our actions. Goals are the specific and measurable steps that we take towards realizing these dreams.

When you were a kid, what did you want to be when you grew up? A doctor? A fireman? A lawyer? Now that you've got some trusty real-world experience under your belt, what aspirations make you excited? Are you gunning for that promotion at work? Is "the world's best mom" a title that you'd love to hear from your kids?

What goals are you working towards? What will you do to celebrate when you reach your goal?

Aspiring to something higher gives our life gusto. Goals keep the energy flowing in the direction of success by giving us results to benchmark our progress. Let's

> If things seem drab and uninspiring, it could be that you have strayed from what you really want to do, from what you were meant to do.

say that you aspire to live a healthy and active lifestyle. Specific goals in the pursuit of this aspiration might include going to the gym three times a week, running a 5K race in three months, or even doing 20 jumping jacks each morning to get into action.

The more committed we are to moving towards our dreams using measurable and achievable goals, the more motivational fire we will have under the seat of our pants. Hot stuff!

Make a list of the aspirations that get you moving today:

What goals have you set to move you along the path towards accomplishment?

What will you do to celebrate the next achievement? Make it fun!

You now understand more clearly the values by which you live (if you didn't already) and the degree to which you abide by this personal creed. You've also described the ambitions that motivate you, along with the goals that you're setting to move you along your path. Now that we've identified the overarching themes of the life that we would like to have, let's look at where we're actually spending our time.

▌ Where You Spend Your Time

The biggest complaint that any of us have is that there isn't enough time in the day. "So much to do, so little time," the popular adage goes. Between family, work, and sleep, what else can we squeeze in? This is often a determining factor in how we approach some new life change—even if it's clear that we need a change.

Your doctor says, "You need to exercise and eat better, your blood pressure is high, and you're definitely at risk for a heart attack."

"Where am I supposed to fit exercise and eating well into the mix?" you say.

Yet when we're forced into submission, by a hospital visit or some other unexpected detour, we take notice. We make time for a change because we see the result of not doing anything staring us in the face.

Take out the work you've done so far throughout this book. Looking first at your vision, then your values, then your aspirations and goals, is there a story emerging? A story of what you most want? A story of the life that is emerging from within you?

Now take out a fresh sheet of paper, or turn to a new page in your journal, and draw the following "A Week in the Life" table. Be sure to make it big enough to include everything you do in a week's time. Fill in the table with what you did in the last week. If you like, you can group your workday like the example at the top of the table (unless you exercise, write, or do some other activity on your lunch break—then include that too).

A WEEK IN THE LIFE			
DAILY ACTIVITIES			HRS SPENT
Sunday	AM	DAY OFF!	
		Breakfast	1
		Beach with kids	3
		Help with homework	2
	PM	Laundry	1
Monday	AM	Exercise/Meditate	0.5
	PM	Work	8
Tuesday	AM		
	PM		
Wednesday	AM		
	PM		
Thursday	AM		
	PM		
Friday	AM		
	PM		
Saturday	AM		
	PM		

To the right of each activity, write the amount of time (in hours) you spent on each activity.

When you are done, answer the following questions:

Where are you spending most of your time?

Is this expenditure of time in alignment with your values, aspirations, and goals? We are looking for areas of opportunity, areas to make space for a great leap forward.

If you spend three hours a day watching TV and no time exercising, yet you value a healthy lifestyle, your day-to-day reality is out of alignment with your value system. This could be a source of stress in your life. Setting a goal around exercising more frequently may help to resolve this stressand open up other areas of your life to a new flow of energy.

Wheel of Life Exercise

The following exercise is one of my favorites for gauging overall satisfaction across several different areas of life.

Use the following page to fill in your own wheel.

Wheel of Life

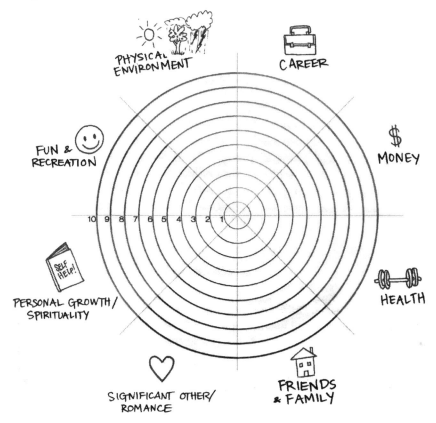

DIRECTIONS: This wheel contains eight sections that, together, represent one way of illustrating the various aspects of your life. This exercise measures your level of satisfaction in each area on the day you work through this exercise.

Taking the center of the wheel as 0 and the outer edge as an ideal 10, rank your level of satisfaction with each life area by drawing a straight or curved line to create a new outer edge (see example). The shape that you see represents your Wheel of Life. How bumpy would the ride be if this were a real wheel?

Example:

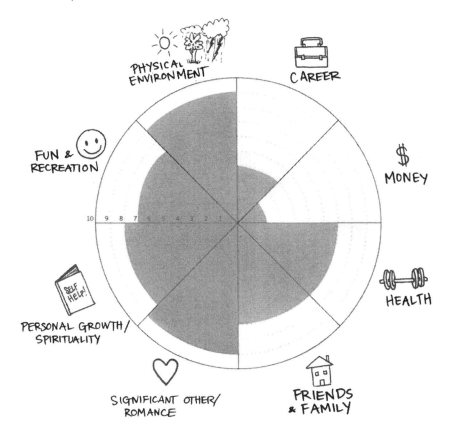

Exploring Your Wheel of Life

What was most telling about this exercise for you? Did anything jump out at you?

If you are experiencing dissatisfaction in some area of life, is this dissatisfaction coming up as stress somewhere? If so, where?

The Wheel of Life, when taken with the other exercises we have done in this section, illustrates in living color where imbalances exist in the way we view our lives. Just like a car driving one thousand miles with a bad wheel, we will eventually break down if we don't allow ourselves to be balanced.

▌ Taking Inventory—Summary

Whoa! We've covered a lot of ground in this last chapter! Flash yourself a smile for the great work you did. Bravo!

You now have a great understanding of your motivating factors. Please take out the following worksheets, or have your journal handy and open to these pages:

Vision for a Life of Less Stress, *pg. 92*

Top Three Values & Rankings, *pg. 97*

Aspirations/Goals List, *pg. 100*

"A Week in the Life" Table, *pg. 102*

Wheel of Life Exercise, *pg. 104*

Looking over all of this, what are you proud of?

What opportunities do you see?

What are you excited about?

Adam Timm

Chapter Nine

"The irony is this: Our bodies react to stress in exactly the same way whether or not we have a good reason for being stressed. The body doesn't care if we're right or wrong. Even in those times when we feel perfectly justified in getting angry—when we tell ourselves it's the healthy response—we pay for it just the same."
—Doc Childre and Howard Martin

Practicing a New Way of Being

Now that we've crafted a vision for the future, looked at what's really important to us, and identified some areas of opportunity, let's explore some practices that will allow this vision to become reality. A life no longer dominated by chronic stress is just around the corner.

True Balance = FREEDOM

The human body and we humans in general are amazingly resilient, adapting to changes on a daily, ongoing basis. As we adapt to change, however, sometimes we don't even realize the stresses under which we are living, having developed our resilience over the course of several years.

Remember the example of Julia, the Type A office manager who quit her overwhelming job to find peace, balance, and a new lease on life waiting for her? Julia didn't always feel claustrophobic, overworked, and constantly stressed about her occupation. In fact there was a time when she enjoyed the challenge, and she enjoyed being part of the creation of an organization that helped improve the lives of students and their parents. But over time, as she took on more and more responsibility and took her work more and more seriously, the scales began to tip to the breaking point.

When we are striding off-balance for too long, something must eventually give. If you've ever walked several miles in bad shoes, you know the toll that instability can wreak on your body. The soreness the next morning is brutal! It is the same way with our minds. Too much focus in one area for too long creates chronic stress, a static of discontentment that we might not even be able to put our finger on. We just know that we're not happy.

When we're living a balanced life, things automatically become easier.

Most of us work entirely too much. Even when we're not at work, there's family, home, friends, and much more to take care of, and suddenly it's time for bed. If we're not working, we're still rushing around doing stuff. Even when we're playing, if we're rushing around like it's a mission, not really allowing ourselves to play, we're simply rolling tour right into our happy playful times too.

We've all taken the family vacation meant to be a break from everything and turned it into a stressed-out ordeal that ended up costing thousands of dollars and leaving us more drained than before we left. This way of relating to "vacation" is widespread.

> **A recent poll found that out of one thousand employees across a wide range of industries, 58 percent reported finding no relief from stress as a result of taking a vacation! And 27 percent reported more stress as a result of the vacation!**

More stress from vacation?! Can you relate?

We have to change our mindset going into these things and adjust our modes of thinking so that everything (including vacation) doesn't create stress.

The Three Dimensions of Being

Stress can arise from being out of balance in any of the following three areas of our being:

MIND   BODY   SPIRIT

Mind

When we are out of balance at the level of the mind, we are constantly on edge.Negative thoughts run rampant and never end. This is the feeling of being your at wit's end— spread too thin, rushed, overwhelmed, and preoccupied.

When the mind is balanced, there is an even flow of our thoughts. That nagging sense of urgency is no longer there. There is a level of confidence in knowing that we are on the right path. It feels like there's more space in all areas of our lives because there is space in our thinking.

Body

When our bodies are out of balance, we feel lethargic, dogged by chronic pain, and prone to injury. We might just feel disconnected from our bodies without really being able to put our finger on why. We might feel weak, run-down, and lazy, yet unable to relax.

When our bodies are balanced, there is strength. Confidence arises from the feeling of being strong and centered in the body. This confidence spills out into other areas of our lives, bringing balance to the mind as well.

Spirit

When we don't feel spiritually balanced there is a feeling of lack. The spark is gone. We might feel like we're simply going through the motions without any direction, wihtout purpose, like we're just a hollow shell.

When we're balanced in spirit, an unwavering sense of purpose exudes from all of our actions. We know that we're on purpose. We are confident in our contributions to the world. There is power, and it is us.

Integration

As we bring one area into balance, the other areas soon follow. If we root ourselves in our spiritual purpose, we naturally see how living in a more balanced body will bring us a greater ability to move towards our personal and spiritual goals. As we bring our bodies into balance, the mind follows as our confidence grows.

We simply need to start where we are. The balance most needed will arrive first, and then we see what else is needed. With awareness, we can understand what is required and then take action.

To cultivate this awareness, we need practices, ways of living that allow us to do so. The follow pages introduce these life-changing practices.

The practices in the following pages have the power to change your life.

When done on a regular basis—daily, when possible—they will provide the foundation for a new life—A life of freedom.

The previous pages helped you craft a vision for this different way of life. The following pages help you put it into action. With regular discipline, these practices become habits, new habits of thinking, being, and doing. Freedom soon follows, freedom from your current habits that keep you locked in a battle with tension and anxiety. Discipline is the key to this freedom.

Chronic stress is truly optional, and the following practices are the gateway to this realization.

Practice Guide

I. The Breath of Freedom

The first practice that we will work with is the Breath of Freedom. In its purest sense, this is nothing other than focused breathing. By creating the time and space simply to do nothing but sit and breathe, we begin to allow a sense of balance to return to our stressed-out existence. We allow for freedom to arrive naturally. If you've already practiced this in the earlier video, awesome! If not, go here: http://www.liveazenlife/breathoffreedom/

Here's the best way to start your own practice: begin by finding a place in your home where it's possible for you to be undisturbed for ten to fifteen minutes. Put your cellphone on silent or in another room. Find a comfortable seat. Set a timer. I suggest starting with ten minutes and working up to twenty minutes per day when you feel ready.

Your posture should be upright, aligned and relaxed, not rigid or slouched. A chair that keeps your back upright works well, or a meditation cushion or meditation bench. The important thing is that you are comfortable and upright, but not so relaxed that you fall asleep.

The Practice

For the next thirty days, commit to this practice daily.

Take a moment to come to rest in your chair. Begin to pay very close attention to the feeling of breathing. Notice the air coming and going, gentle and relaxed. Almost immediately, there is a sensation of the body relaxing, a slight sinking feeling as your body's tension loosens and melts away.

Pay very close attention to the breath at the tip of the nose. Feel the slight coolness of the in breath, the slight warmth of the out breath. Do this now for a few breaths.

See how closely you can feel the breath at the tip of the nose. See if you can notice the exact point where the breath enters the nostrils. Do you feel it more on the right or the left side? Maybe you feel the coolness of the breath in the back of the throat, or even down further, into your lungs. Allow your attention to fall squarely on the breath. Let the mind become one with the feeling of the breath.

If you notice your mind wandering, that's ok. Each time you notice yourself caught in thinking, just bring your attention back to the breath. You can let the thoughts dissolve, or fly away, or simply move along without a care. The thoughts are like clouds passing in the sky—no connection, no worries.

Any time the mind wanders, we simply come back to the breath. Even if we have to do this fifty times in this session, it's ok. This is the practice. Simply return to the breath, again and again, in a gentle and non-judgmental way, without any comments, without any additional thoughts.

As the mind begins to settle, the frequency of thoughts slows down. See if you can rest in this space between the thoughts. Rest in this stillness, watching the breath, feeling the rise and fall of the chest, and the expansion of the abdomen, just being one with the breath.

Sit, breathing like this, for ten minutes each day. This practice alone has the power to change your life.

Notes on Cultivating the Breath of Freedom

When we connect the mind with the breath, the mind becomes one with the present moment. The breath is happening *now*.

> When we use the breath as the focal point, we bring our attention, which is normally caught up in future expectation and past conditioning, back to the moment. The practice is about returning again and again to this moment.

In the present moment, there is no stress. Through this practice, we put the thinking mind in neutral, and simply let everything else go. Everything. We let our thoughts go, unattached. We let our plans and agendas go. We let our physical tension relax and melt away. We just fall into the moment, returning to a true experience of what's going on inside of us.

> Sometimes this practice feels like it brings up more anxiety, more tension, more stress. But what's actually happening is a bit more hopeful. We are becoming more attuned to the feeling of the stress we carry around with us each day.
>
> We are waking up.

We notice baseline of anxiety that we normally carry around with us every day. And with this awareness, we can choose to relax and let go.

Lessons from the Breath of Freedom

1. This is an invitation to slow down. The Breath of Freedom is just that, freeing us from our conditioned reactions. It offers us the

opportunity to sit down and do ione *thing* at a time: watch the breath. We don't have to rush around. We don't have to do anything. This is huge. So much of our stress and discontent comes from running around without thinking about why we're actually doing it. Through meditation we find that we don't have to think about it. We can just let it go.

2. Doing nothing isn't boring. With regular practice, we see that not only is doing nothing not boring, it gives us the perspective to see what's going on in our lives. We can look forward to our meditation time as time to unplug, release, and recharge.

3. Stress is not of this moment. The Breath of Freedom allows us to sit in the present moment where there is peace and stillness. The thinking mind gets to take a break, and we can relax the mental and physical tension that comes with all our thoughts. Thoughts are of some other time—future expectation, past conditioning—and when the mind is one with the breath, there is no room for thought. No room for anything other than the feeling of the present moment: the feeling of the body breathing.

To de-stress any time:

Whenever you need to, take three long, deep breaths, feeling your abdomen expand with each inhale. On the exhale, feel your tension release, visualizing any tension that you might be aware of simply melting down into the earth. Inhale, feel the abdomen expand, exhale, feel yourself relax as the tension loosens and melts downward.

Use this whenever you need to—in the car, at work, at home—and feel the stress and tension melt away.

II. Journaling

Another powerful practice that helps us to see our reflexive patterns of thought is journaling, or self-reflection. In our journal, we write down thoughts and observations about our lives, engaging in a discussion around what's going on, and what it means. With this practice, we document our unfolding journey.

Example:

9/13/14

What a gift, this life. The last few days have been truly powerful, with life's momentum flowing in the direction of my dreams. I write these words to bring more awareness of my thoughts, and to document this unfolding journey. Onward!

The Practice

For the first thirty days, commit to writing every day—even if you have nothing to say. This will establish the habit of self-reflection. And remember, you are writing for no audience. This is only for you.

As the days go by and your meditation practice begins to take hold, you will notice moments when you used to do one thing (through a reflexive pattern of worn-out thinking), but now you're choosing to do something different. Be sure to write the details down in your journal. Celebrate these breaks from the old norm! There will be many more.

As you contemplate the deeper meaning of these changes for your life of less stress and more joy, be sure to spell out these unfolding thoughts, these unfolding visions for a brighter tomorrow that is already here.

As your positive thoughts inform your words, your actions will soon follow. Journaling fosters this singularity of purpose by reflecting the changes as they occur.

▌ III. Nutrition

The importance of eating healthy cannot be overstated. When we neglect to nourish our bodies with the nutrients needed to live powerfully happy lifestyles, we are sabotaging this happiness before it can even take root.

So many of us eat only because we have to—what a nuisance! We'd rather not eat if it would mean an extra few hours in the day. This perspective on eating leads us to make poor choices when it comes to deciding what to put in our bodies: Fast food. Delivery pizza. Frozen ready-made options. Whatever is the quickest, give it to me.

There are those who are locked into the "whatever's quickest/easiest" loop. Pasta, Hot Pockets, greasy Mexican food every day. Lots of breads. No vegetables. And if a vegetable does make it into the diet, it's the same one every day.

We eat an overabundance of heavily processed foods. Enriched bleached flour is a staple ingredient. High fructose corn syrup abounds. Refined sugars or sugar substitutes are everywhere. Unaware of the harm we are doing to our bodies that's eroding our ability to live well, we are motivated more by cost than anything else. But besides the dollars, what is the true cost?

When we don't feed the cells in our bodies with the proper nutrients to sustain a vibrant life, we wilt, just like a flower in the mid-day sun. It's no wonder that we feel lethargic and off-balance when we don't take measures to fuel the lifestyles we pursue. Without feeding our cells a balanced diet rich in a variety of fresh foods we are out of balance at the cellular level! How can we hope to live stress-free when we are stressing our bodies to the core?

Stress and Nutrition

Aside from what we eat, there's the matter of how we eat. Are you motivated by fear to eat healthy? As Marc David of the Institute for the Psychology of Eating says, "When we eat something because we're afraid we'll get sick or fat if we don't eat it, what we're really doing is feeding our fear. When fear is the motivation, fear will also be the end result."

Eating while we're mentally stressed or emotionally wound up usually leads us to eat more. As discussed in the earlier section on stress response and digestion, we are physically unable to digest our food and absorb its nutrients when we are stressed out. Do you find yourself rushing through your meals so you can get to the next thing? That's stressful!

If we aren't aware, this mind-body connection prevents us from receiving the nutrients we need, further stressing us out. To cut the stress, we need to change the way we eat.

▌ The Practice

WHAT TO EAT

For the next thirty days, choose to eat a diet with as many organic foods as possible. Eat a variety of organic vegetables with lots of dark green leafy veggies such as kale, spinach, and bok choi. Eat few or no refined sugars (no high fructose corn syrup), and no caffeine. If you feel withdrawal symptoms as a result of cutting the sugar and caffeine, use them very sparingly.

Limit your carbohydrate intake. Opt for as many whole grains as you can. When you look on the ingredient label for a loaf of bread that says 100% Whole Wheat, but has enriched wheat flour as an ingredient, choose a different brand.

Limit your intake of red meat, and if you do need to eat meat, opt for organic, free-range chicken. Get your protein from organic legumes, like kidney, pinto, black, and garbanzo beans instead. Switch to organic eggs. Cut out processed foods like frozen and fast foods.

Reduce your calorie intake to 2,000 calories per day for women, and 2,250 calories per day for men.

For a quick chart of the difference between conventional and organic farming, check the following website from the Mayo Clinic: http://www.mayoclinic.com/health/organic-food/NU00255/

How to Eat

For the next thirty days choose to eat in a more relaxed way than you usually do. Take a moment before each meal to catch your breath, say a word of gratitude, and to notice the texture and the smell of the food in front of you.

As you eat, take your time. Chew your food twice as slowly as normal. Notice the taste and texture in your mouth. Allow yourself to enjoy your meal. Enjoying and savoring our food activates the relaxation response and gives us maximum digestive power.

IV. Exercise

Just as we need the right nutrients, without regular exercise the body slowly deteriorates. Now, it's not necessary to hit the gym for two hours or to run ten miles every day. We're talking about balance. What's important is that you start doing something *today*.

You may feel like you don't have the energy for this, or like you don't have time. But this is part of the thinking that keeps us locked in to the stress cycle. It will get better in time. The amazing thing about the body is that the more you use it, the more energy it produces! As you feel your level of endurance and strength increase, the results will fuel you to continue.

▌ The Practice

For the next thirty days, commit to twenty minutes of aerobic exercise five days a week (walking, jogging, running, spinning class, step aerobics), and twenty minutes of stretching/flexibility exercise (yoga or something similar), two days/week.

As the body is allowed to move and enjoy an increased level of activity, ielevated levels of oxygenated blood enhance the body's natural defenses. Endorphins are also released, fighting stress hormones and increasing our feelings of well-being.

Each day you exercise, document in your journal what type of activity you did, and how long you engaged in it. Monitor your results to see how quickly your fitness level improves.

▌ V. Play

What do you do to celebrate your daily wins? How do you reward yourself for a job well done? What have you done to play lately?

The best example of play is something from childhood— Those long summer days when you were simply lost in whatever you were doing, oblivious to time, immersed in the fun and joy of simply being. As we grow into adulthood and become absorbed by the responsibilities that come along with it, we forget to play. We forget to forget our serious selves for an afternoon and let go. We need these moments of downtime. Play is essential for the balance we seek.

If we go too long without play, our spirits become dampened, our mind gets frazzled. Our short, angry fuse reveals the level of stress that we carry.

Play can include anything that brings you joy: A camping trip with the kids, or solo. A bike ride around town. A trip to the beach. A walk around the block with the dog. A leisurely cup of tea on the front step, my personal favorite. Joy and contentment are the key.

The Practice

For the next thirty days, at least once a day, allow yourself a moment of play, a moment to lose yourself in whatever you're doing. Simply let go. Schedule this time for yourself. It can be with a loved one or a friend, but it is really about you. If this time with someone else might turn into a discussion or something more serious than playing, then go by yourself. Dare to be selfish (call it self-caring), if only this once.

Allowing the Practices to Inform Your Life

In just two weeks of daily practice, your life will begin to change at a fundamental level. After thirty days, you may never go back to your old, stressed-out life.

Using meditation as our guide, we relax into life, into the way things are. We see the things we can change, and we take bold action. We no longer worry about what is not in our control.

We open to less resistant ways of thinking and being. We relax the worn patterns that once held us captive. We become more compassionate, more genuine, less reactive.

As balanced living becomes the focus, we trust our newfound, unwavering instinct about life. Where there was once fear and uncertainty, there ispower.

When we aren't dominated by stress, we can see clearly.

The practices have brought us awareness. With awareness we have reached understanding. This understanding has given us the ground for action.

> Where there was once fear and uncertainty, there is now power.

This is no less than a cure. A cure for the Type A personality. A cure for stress that kills. A cure for the panicky anxiety that prevents true joy from ever shining through. What a relief!

I invite you to make these practices a way of life. I invite you to show them to others. Spread the good news!

Adam Timm

Epilogue

"Don't underestimate the value of doing nothing, of just going along, listening to all the things you can't hear, and not bothering."
—Pooh's Little Instruction Book

▎Stress is Optional!

Over the course of human history, we have come to respond to the stressors in our environment in a certain way. These feelings of stress have ensured the survival of our species. Without responding to very real threats of danger instinctually, the human race might have ceased to exist past the days of the dreaded saber-toothed tiger.

We carry this powerful machinery into the present day. The same mechanism that allowed our ancestors to thrive in the wilderness now puts us at risk of a host of chronic conditions and diseases. Stress, (not the saber-toothed tiger), is now the enemy.

To fight this enemy, we can only do it alone, for it is an enemy of our own creation. Stress begins and ends in your mind just as it did in my mind. In order to fight chronic stress, we must change the way we think. We must adopt more relaxed ways of thinking, being, and doing that interrupt the ancient instinct of fight or flight.

To arrive at this more relaxed way, we must take action. The awareness of our stressed state is the first step, but this consciousness of our state alone only gets us so far. We need to experience a new way of living, outside of our conditioned reflexes.

> We need to experience a new way of living, outside of our conditioned reflexes.

The simple practices contained in this book will provide a pathway to take our burgeoning awareness and turn it into action. But we must start on faith. We have to start with the vision of a less stressful future and the faith that we have the power to bring this vision into being. It takes faith in ourselves, coupled with a drive to succeed. Success is a life outside of the pain that has become normal for us.

Once we experience the difference, there is no turning back. Just thirty days of practice can take you beyond this turning point. Commit to it. Allow it to become your way of life, your way of thinking, acting, and being.

With inspired action and discipline, you too will realize the truth of the phrase "Stress Is Optional." Without the stress, life doesn't feel like work anymore. Then we can do nothing, and be okay with it, just like Pooh said.

> Once we experience the difference, there is no turning back. Just thirty days of practice can take you beyond this turning point. Commit to it. Allow it to become your way of life, your way of thinking, acting, and being.

For a final thought from Adam:

http://www.liveazenlife.com/finalthought

Adam Timm

Bibliography

1. Perlmutter, D., & Villoldo, A. "How Stress Harms the Brain." Power up Your Brain: The Neuroscience of Enlightenment. Carlsbad, CA: Hay House, 2011. 59. Print.

2. Hanson, R. & Mendius, R. "Why Aren't People Happier?" On Meditations to Change Your Brain [CD] Boulder, CO: Sounds True, 2009

3. Ibid.

4. Perlmutter, op. cit. 59.

5. Ray, R. A. "Core Teachings." Indestructible Truth: The Living Spirituality of Tibetan Buddhism. Boston: Shambhala, 2002. 230. Print.

6. Perlmutter, D., & Villoldo, A. "Neural Networks and Habits of the Mind." Power up Your Brain: The Neuroscience of Enlightenment. Carlsbad, CA: Hay House, 2011. 46. Print.

7. Hoffman, B., & Deitch, J. "Stress." Discover Wellness: How Staying Healthy Can Make You Rich. Apple Valley, MN: Center Path Pub., 2007. 66. Print.

8. Donnan, G. A., Fisher, M., Macleod, M., & Davis, S. M. (May 2008). "Stroke." Lancet 371 (9624): 1612–23. doi:10.1016/S0140-6736(08)60694-7. Internet, PubMed.gov; PMID 18468545.

9. Dorland, W. A. Newman. "Coronary Artery Disease." Dorland's Illustrated Medical Dictionary. Philadelphia, PA: Saunders, 2011. 371. Print.

10. Thomas, A. C., Knapman, P. A., Krikler, D. M., Davies, M. J. (December 1988). "Community study of the causes of 'natural' sudden death". BMJ 297 (6661): 1453–6.doi:10.1136/bmj.297.6661.1453. Internet, PubMed.gov; PMC 1835183. PMID 3147014.

11. Rosamond, W., Flegal, K., Friday, G., Furie, K., Go, A., Greenlund, K., Haase, N., Ho, M., Howard, V., Kissela, B., Kittner, S., Lloyd-Jones, D., McDermott, M., Meigs, J., Moy, C., Nichol, G., O'Donnell, C.J., Roger, V., Rumsfeld, J., Sorlie, P., Steinberger, J., Thom, T., Wasserthiel-Smoller, S., & Hong, Y. (February 2007). "Heart Disease and Stroke Statistics—2007 update." American Heart Association Statistics Committee and Stroke Statistics Subcommittee. Circulation 115 (5): e69–171

12. Ibid.

13. Khansari, D., Murgo, A., & Faith, R. (1990). "Effects of stress on the immune system." Immunology Today, 11, 170–175.

14. Kemeny, M. E. (2007). "Understanding the interaction between psychosocial stress and immune-related diseases: A stepwise progression." Brain, Behavior, and Immunity, 21 (8), 1009–1018.

15. Hanson, R. The stress response. On Stress-Proof Your Brain. [CD] Boulder, CO: Sounds True, 2010

16. Parkad, C.R., Campbella, A.M., & Diamond, D.M. (2001). "Chronic psychosocial stress impairs learning and memory and increases sensitivity to yohimbine in adult rats." Biological Psychology, 50, 994-1004.

17. McGowan, K. (April 2008). "Second Nature." Psychology Today , 74.

18. Boyce, B. (March 2012). "Taking the Measure of Mind." Shambala Sun, 59.

About the Author

A former road-rager and retired 911 operator from the Los Angeles Police Department, Adam is here to help you kick your nasty habit of stressing out every day. An operator for over a decade, he suffered for years in exhausting relationships, chronically stressed, before final kicking his own habit. Adam believes that anyone can attain a life of peace, joy, and freedom, without quitting their job, selling their kids, or hiding under a rock.

Adam is a certified stress management consultant, corporate trainer, and workshop facilitator. He lives in Los Angeles, the most stressful city in America, with his stress-free cat, Koala. He enjoys sitting on his front steps, chatting with neighbors, and sipping his morning tea.

For more information on upcoming events and programs, visit Adam at www.LiveaZenLife.com.

Ready to Breathe Easy Again and Have More "Me" Time?

Take the next step now.

COMPLIMENTARY DISCOVERY SESSION: (value $200)

Tired of being stressed out? Want to go deeper with practices you learned here? Your Freedom Coach will help you get clear on your vision for a life with less stress, and give you specific action steps to get there. The session could be the turning point towards your life of FREEDOM.

Complete your application here:

www.liveazenlife.com/discoverysession

We look forward to speaking with you!

Made in the USA
Middletown, DE
05 November 2015